TRANSATLANTIC BETRAYAL

THE RB211 AND THE DEMISE
OF ROLLS-ROYCE LTD

ANDREW PORTER

AMBERLEY

To Francesca and Annabelle

Europe can look the Americans straight in the eyes.

Sir Denning Pearson.
Chief Executive,
Rolls-Royce Ltd.

Front and back cover images courtesy of the Royal Aeronautical Society.

First published 2013

Amberley Publishing
The Hill, Stroud
Gloucestershire, GL5 4EP

www.amberley-books.com

British Library Cataloguing in Publication Data.
A catalogue record for this book is available from the British Library.

ISBN 978 1 4456 0649 1

Typeset in 10pt on 12pt Sabon.
Typesetting and Origination by Amberley Publishing.
Printed in the UK.

CONTENTS

Rolls-Royce RB.211 22B. (Author)

Whittle W2/700. (Author)

PREFACE
THE CASE FOR ROLLS-ROYCE AND AIRBUS –
TIME, METHOD AND MOTIVES

Time

As a schoolboy I was smitten by the aviation bug and because of my fascination with aircraft, I was knowledgeable of the differences between a RB.211, a CF6 and a JT9D. However, it was to be much later in life before I would seriously investigate the structural differences between these engines. The inclination to investigate occurred to me with regard to the Airbus A300B, the Lockheed L-1011, and the McDonnell Douglas DC-10 engine nacelles: could there be a connection between these three apparently unique commercial aircraft, apart from the shared utilization of the then new high by-pass ratio turbofan aero-engine? From my observation of the intriguing similarities between jet engine nacelle designs which were utilized by the aircraft manufacturers on their respective aircraft that were designed in the 1960s, there came the motivation to seriously investigate the aero-engine technology.

Method

I started to search and through my investigations, of government reports, scientific papers, journals, newspaper articles and the works of respected industry advisors and historians of aviation, I have found substantial evidence which appears to link the three aforementioned projects.

My investigations followed a series of seemingly unrelated events, which as these events unfolded in the context of the time, suggests there existed tangible and higher connections between the different projects. Continuing the search, my investigation revealed that the three-quarter-length nacelle/pod design and the related technologies, with which Short Brothers Ltd was contracted to supply the Rolls-Royce-designed nacelle for the RB.211, were sought after by the US Rohr Industries Corporation, for use on the CF6-powered McDonnell Douglas DC-10. Further investigation revealed that Rohr and McDonnell Douglas would subsequently employ the nacelle and power-plant technologies on the GE-engined DC-10 and, according to a very highly regarded French industrialist, the technologies were the same as those used on the Rolls-Royce RB.211.

Subsequent to the use of the similar technologies on the DC-10, McDonnell Douglas would manage the supply of the DC-10 engine pod and nacelle as a power-plant package

Airbus A.300B. (RAeS)

with the General Electric CF6 engine for use on the European Airbus A.300B. This is all the more interesting because the original engine power-plant selected by Airbus for the initial A.300 was the Rolls-Royce RB.207. The Rolls-Royce RB.207 design had the same power-plant nacelle design features and technologies as the other members of the Rolls-Royce advanced technology aero-engine family such as the RB.203 Trent and the RB.211 for the Lockheed L1011 Tristar.

The linkages I have identified appear to establish what might be termed as an interdependent crossover or sharing of power-plant technologies concerning the engine mounting and engine pod/nacelle. The technology crossover, or sharing, appears to have occurred between the UK and the US at a time when the then Labour government was setting the aviation agenda in the UK and pushing Rolls-Royce Limited to secure an American outlet for its advanced technology RB.211 high bypass ratio aero-engine. At the same time in the US, Secretary for Defense Robert McNamara was driving through drastic political changes in the US aviation procurement process, which were designed to redistribute the balance of power in favour of the White House. The investigation of shared, or interdependent political, industrial and technological strategies for aviation at an international level also appear to have informed Harold Wilson's Labour government in its dealings with its French and German partners in connection with Airbus. Labour, as the holder of the purse strings controlling UK government Launch Aid, would pressure Rolls-Royce to co-develop the advanced technology engine for powering the European Airbus collaborative effort, while insisting a scaled effort was put into a smaller engine for the US market.

Motives

The projected superior operating performance of the RB.203, RB.207 and RB.211 Advanced Technology aero-engines, in relation to their competitors, was provided by an inherently superior aero-engine design. Airlines and aircraft manufacturers generally acknowledged that the Rolls-Royce ATE engine family would sweep the board for powering a second generation of wide/body, feeder-liner and air bus aircraft. Such a prospect for the Rolls-Royce revolutionary three-shaft high by-pass aero-engines meant that Rolls-Royce Limited significantly threatened the commercial prospects of the competing US engine manufacturers, which had alone dominated the world's commercial market for piston aero-engines before the advent of the jet engine/gas turbine.

With all the implied consequences that Rolls-Royce Limited's challenge would have for the US aerospace and aero-engine industries, in areas such as aero-engine sales, finance, employment, balance of trade and international prestige, the foreign RB.211 high by-pass turbofan aero-engine was too great a threat for the US Administration, and its powerfully linked interest groups to ignore. After American Airlines had publicly indicated that it had chosen the RB.211 to power its order for the DC-10 in 1968, a powerful force of US political and industrial interests were harnessed to counter the foreign invasion.

From the UK Labour government's perspective, its policy of financial support for Rolls-Royce was focused on the RB.211 and the engine's specific potential in the US market. However, on revisiting historical sources it seems that the then UK Labour government appears to have duped Rolls-Royce Limited into acting as an intelligence gatherer and this appears to have resulted in the company being used, unwittingly, as a bargaining tool ultimately for influencing a favourable US-led IMF deal in support of the UK Labour government. This book provides an insight into a possible theory of a politically inspired strategy of over-reach designed ultimately to bring about the over-all demise of Rolls-Royce Limited in particular and the UK aviation industry in general.

Some Observations of Possible Outcomes

The central focus of this work is to revisit a major historic event in UK, US and European aviation history. This work will examine recent and previously unpublished evidence, among other accessible sources relating to the event, and judge whether the new materials warrant an inclusion or adjustment to the received view and then to draw political, social and economic lessons from a synthesis of the materials.

The major historic event that this work will examine is the significant breakthrough made by Rolls-Royce Limited, in 1968, into the massive US commercial aviation market. The breakthrough into the US market was made possible because of the UK company's revolutionary three-shaft RB.211 high by-pass ratio turbofan technology aero-engine.

Recently published evidence, which was hitherto publicly un-accessible, seems to offer up the possibility of a significant shift in the received view of UK, European and US aviation history. With the advent of the latest communications revolution provided by the internet, the new evidence has generally become available in the public domain. It is because of such reasons as the increased availability of information online and the massive growth in historical knowledge via the internet that the author suggests a review of the history of the development of the high by-pass ratio aero-engine technology RB.211 is both warranted and necessary.

In the author's view, the establishment of a new synthesis would challenge the existing received views by established aviation historians such as Boyne, Newhouse, Jackson, and

Heppenheimer, and add support for the works of Gunston, Pugh, Lawrence and Thornton. This work would then provide those with an interest in aviation history with an additional understanding of events and of the contextual political and economic reasons relating to them. Similarly, a revised work may provide a greater degree of understanding for persons interested in following economic history to challenge or support the works of academics such as Lawrence and Thornton, Bowden, and Lazonick and Prencipe.

The questions which will arise from this investigation will be numerous and, as has already been indicated in a limited sense, will cover a broad spectrum of interests. However, the fundamental address of this work must, I believe, be that a great injustice has been inflicted on the brave and loyal men and women who once proudly worked in Britain's aviation industries, of which a review of the history of the RB.211 would provide a corrective insight. Such a review could tie in with a revision of Britain's apparent history of managerial and industrial incompetence and the country's so called technological downfall, stories which, it seems, were reiterated and exacerbated by a treacherous cabal who, in this instance, politically orchestrated the denial of economic markets.

I believe that in the light of recent European political developments, a revision of aviation history would add to the received European view. A revised European view of aviation history would, as well as providing historical accuracy in contrast to Newhouse's and Heppenheimer's version of events, mean that once again in relation to the future of aviation trade, in Sir Denning's words: 'Europe can look the Americans straight in the eyes.'

INTRODUCTION
WHY RE-WRITE HISTORY?

The Importance of History: The Over-Reach of Rolls-Royce Limited

Historical sources suggest that on occasions when US interests wanted to gain aviation technology from their UK ally, it appears that they forged political and industrial organizational alliances with similarly positioned UK interests and companies to collaborate, technically, on strategically interdependent projects. Having gained an alignment of interests and access to the company hosting the technology, it appears that politically inspired mechanisms were then set in motion to bring about the collapse of the host company both financially and technically through an applied strategy of over-reach.

The assumed objective of applying the political strategy of over-reach to the host company was to bring about the collapse of a duplicated interdependent effort, and to remove the threats of technical and commercial competition once the gained technology was employed on similar US projects. Such a strategy would have been in line with an Anglo-US policy of non-duplicated effort for projects in the strategically important aviation industry.

With the election of the Wilson Labour government in 1964, and its publicly stated commitment to address what it perceived were the excesses of the UK aviation industry, it appears that the US had a natural ally in the Wilson Labour government since Labour was politically committed to the demise of the UK aviation industry. One argument for the removal of the competitive and technical threats posed by the UK aviation industry was that such a prospect would have been very welcome among US aviation interests.

The Wilson government harboured policies towards the UK aviation industry which focused on reducing the apparent wastefulness of a British industry that seemingly produced uneconomic aircraft when compared to the US and duplicated the production of similar US aircraft and engines. According to Labour politicians, the UK wasted its limited resources on duplicated efforts trying to achieve ambitious projects. In an industry that was seen by the anti-aviation MPs as un-necessary and a publicly funded featherbed of excess, such efforts wastefully took up valuable strategic resources whereas, some argued, supposedly similar US products, which addressed similar UK needs, could be purchased more economically and on time from US sources.

In contrast to the aforementioned political assertions made by members of the Labour government who argued in favour of US-produced equipment, this work highlights a case where the political reasons given for the compromising of UK-sourced technical and engineering solutions were far removed from the factually supported reality.

A Twist in the Tale

In the United States, a government-sponsored high by-pass technology development and production program conflicted with US commercial interests. The result was the production of two high by-pass ratio aero-engines: the US government-sponsored General Electric TF39 for the US military Lockheed C-5A and the Pratt & Whitney JT9D for the commercial Boeing 747. Yet, despite the publicly stated strategic intentions of non-duplication between the inter-dependent US and UK governments, Rolls-Royce was encouraged by political and industrial interests on both sides of the Atlantic to develop its revolutionary three-shaft advanced high by-pass aero-engine technology. In response, Rolls-Royce would bind itself politically and stake its future on its revolutionary ATE family of aero-engines, of which the RB.211 would eventually compete directly against the US engines.

The financial encouragement for Rolls-Royce to develop the advanced RB.211 aero-engine came in the form of Launch Aid from the UK government. From the US, the spur was the promise of large orders for US air buses from US airlines. Another incentive was the prospect of the company controlling the design, development and supply of the entire power-plant. Yet another point of encouragement was the prospect of a fully developed high by-pass ratio aero-engine, with the development costs fully paid for by US sales, which would then have been made available for use on a European airbus. Such a manoeuvre by Rolls-Royce to sell its engine design for use by the US airlines would have effectively released the European Airbus consortium from the high costs of engine development. This would have benefited the European Airbus consortium and enabled the Europeans to have competitively priced the A.300. Tellingly, perhaps, the development and export of Rolls-Royce's high by-pass aero-engine technologies would ameliorate US technological weaknesses through direct purchase. (Hayward 1976)

The most prominent and ardent political advocate of Rolls-Royce's push for US business was the Minister for Technology, Anthony Wedgwood Benn. It was Benn, as the Labour Minister, who had responsibility for overseeing any agreements between the UK government and Rolls-Royce when the company required financial assistance from the government in the form of Launch Aid. An indication of the Minister's interest in UK aviation can be observed from a look at the history of the then Labour government's involvement with the Anglo-French Concorde.

A summary of the Labour government's involvement would indicate that it tried several times to cancel the Anglo-French Concorde programme but because of strong French resistance and a probable £140 million penalty, the Labour government's attempts were aborted. The Labour government had to acquiesce and allow the Sovereign strategic programme to continue, while feigning support for the aircraft. As Minister for Technology, Benn's only chance of getting rid of Concorde, besides hoping that the aircraft would crash on to the *QE2* and therefore cause a national disaster, was to wait for Concorde to fail technically. Had Concorde failed technically then Benn could probably have withdrawn the United Kingdom from the Anglo-French programme and, along with the associated public furore over wasted taxpayers' money spent on a technical failure, could have probably done so without the fear of French legal reprisal.

Strategic Vision

On 29 November 1962, Amery and de Corcel signed the agreement for '...the Development and Production of a Civil Supersonic Transport Aircraft' on behalf of their respective nations of Great Britain and the French Republic. In doing so, they understood they were committing Great Britain and France to a contract to achieve a long-term strategic vision, and to emphasise the certain fulfilment of the Sovereign strategy there was no cancellation clause.

Detractors of the Anglo-French contract for the long term strategic vision, among them numerous US and UK politicians, business managers and academic observers, openly criticised the so called 'white elephant' project. An American academic working for the US public health service had an article published in an American law journal where he expressed his disbelief in the British and French decision to proceed with Concorde: '[The decision] may never be fully understood, especially in light of the heavy criticism the [Concorde] continues to receive...'. (Nelson 1969)

The detractors, like the American health official, took delight in pouring scorn on what appeared to them an obviously flawed contract that had locked both nations into the total development of the revolutionary Anglo-French SST Concorde. Perhaps persons of a similarly negative disposition were so inclined because they lacked determination and vision? Such persons would probably have derided the determined efforts made by Whittle in establishing the jet engine. They would probably have poured scorn on the revolutionary social benefits the drastic jet engine technology was to bring, for example, to commercial aviation. Commercial passengers in the new jet age were to benefit from the time shrinking advantages offered by jet-propelled aircraft over and above the technically limited, old and cumbersome piston-engined craft.

The world's first jet airliner, the de Havilland Comet, profoundly changed international air travel in 1952. Airline passengers who travelled on the Comet arrived at their destinations sooner, in aircraft that flew more smoothly above the weather. BOAC's Comets provided these benefits to its fare paying customers while increasing numbers of economists contemplated how cost-efficiently the big US manufacturers produced their technologically outdated piston-engined aeroplanes.

Amery and de Courcel mirrored the determination of the British and French nations to succeed with Concorde in international aviation. I argue that they were gifted with the far-sighted strategic vision of the benefits which the development of the Concorde SST would

BAC/Aérospatiale
Concorde.

de Havilland Comet.

bring to Great Britain and France. At its political and industrial inception, the aircraft that would be subsequently named the Concorde was projected to have a similarly profound impact on air travel in the 1970s and beyond as did the revolutionary de Havilland Comet jet airliner when the world's first passenger jet was introduced to service in 1952.

In contrast, Benn and the Wilson Labour government left no stone unturned as they desperately tried to renege on the Anglo-French agreement and to cancel a technological lynchpin in the battle with the US for the control of the skies.

An Advantageous Position

A similar convergence of political and technical circumstances seems to have repeated itself with Rolls-Royce Limited. Rolls-Royce in the 1960s was in a similar situation in that its revolutionary high bypass aero-engine technology for the new wide-body air bus commercial transports was a generation ahead of its US competitors. The high bypass aero-engine was set to revolutionize passenger air travel, and having command over the advanced high bypass aero-engine technologies would mean control over aircraft performance and control over which airframe company could apply it. The Rolls-Royce company's advanced aero-engine technology placed it in an advantageous position relative to its US competitors. However, politically it placed the company on a projected collision course in relation to UK-US strategic interdependence.

In 1965/66, collaborative European projects, which would utilize the new high bypass aero-engine technologies, were gaining political and industrial momentum. It was during this period that the European Airbus A.300 was conceived. The Airbus design promoted advanced European aviation technologies and underlined the significance of the collaborative European effort in the face of US airborne colonization. The Rolls-Royce high bypass aero-engine was one of two critical technologies that enabled the Europeans to promote the superior Airbus A.300 design against less efficient US aircraft.

Critical Junction

It is within the light of this critical junction of US and European aviation history that I assert in this work that the Labour Minister Anthony Wedgwood Benn and the Wilson Labour government employed interdependent political and economic strategies for the manipulation of Rolls-Royce Limited.

For economic reasons, Benn pointed Rolls-Royce in the direction of the US to enable Rolls-Royce to gain Launch Aid for its revolutionary high bypass aero-engine technology. The potential of great riches, which the grand images of the enormous American aviation market conjured up, was a powerful inducement and it is probable that Benn used such images to encourage the directors of Rolls-Royce to accept his Ministry's strategy.

A consequence of Benn's insistence of linking Launch Aid to the development of the RB.211, an aero-engine programme that was centrally focused on gaining business in the US market, was that the RB.211 programme's outcomes were insidiously and inextricably linked to the health of the whole company. Ultimately, the Launch Aid package that the Wilson Labour government championed and financed for the RB.211 became pivotal in determining the future of the whole of Rolls-Royce Limited.

Political encouragement and scientific support were provided to design and develop Rolls-Royce's revolutionary aero-engine technologies to the point where they sucked in most of Rolls-Royce's resources. The commitment of significant finances in support of research, development and the build up of substantial production resources would stretch Rolls-Royce Ltd but such a commitment was a calculated risk. However, a wind-shear supply change took the financial risks beyond even the eminent capabilities of Rolls-Royce Limited. Notwithstanding the last minute change in airframe supply, I suggest that the critical factor in determining the overall outcome for Rolls-Royce Limited was the onerous US Lockheed contract for the RB.211. Rolls-Royce was to be constrained by the compressed time frame limits, which were imposed by the Total Package Procurement-style contracts, as drawn up by Lockheed under New York law. The culminating bang of these effects would leave Rolls-Royce Limited fatally exhausted; the contrived cycle complete.

The Labour government appear to have been fully supportive of these positions, and to have afforded the Rolls-Royce company every assistance in its American efforts. Strategically, it appears that Rolls-Royce Limited was to be restrained to the point of financial failure and technically, because of the impossible conditions and timescales imposed by Lockheed, Rolls-Royce was to be constrained and therefore exposed to the harsh and unfriendly realities of the rigorously imposed and rigidly enforced commercial contractual penalties under New York law.

The UK Labour government placed great emphasis on the economic concerns relating to the financial viability of the Rolls-Royce company's high by-pass aero-engine programme. Their concerns were important to an extent but equally if not more important to the company were the technical issues which allowed Rolls-Royce to provide an advanced range of aero-engines with superior operating performance. The post-merger Rolls-Royce was ahead of its US contemporaries on a number of high by-pass aero-engine technologies. Therefore, the relative comparisons made by the Labour government showing the UK to be behind its US competitors in terms of productivity and efficiency were almost meaningless.

Serious Threat

The US engine companies were possibly ahead of their learning curve relative to the development of their high by-pass aero-engine technology, but significantly, the Rolls-Royce company's knowledge of high bypass ratio aero-engine technologies was a generation ahead of the US DoD-supported HBR programs. This position is, after all, borne out by the fact that it would be the Rolls-Royce-designed and developed advanced HBR technologies which would persuade the US political and industrial interests to import the Rolls-Royce RB.211 high bypass aero-engine for installation on their wide bodied aircraft. That the Rolls-Royce company was in a strong technical position relative to its US competitors is also borne out by the reactions of US political and industrial interests. These US interests made out that the proposed import of the foreign Rolls-Royce ATE aero-engines was considered to be such a serious threat to US national interests that the issue became embroiled in a public battle that played out all the way up to the US president in the White House.

In relation to the respective merits of the technical positions of the UK and the US in advanced aero-engine technologies, the Labour government appears at first glance to have paid little regard to the long term commercial advantages the UK's technical lead would have had over its competitors and what the advantageous position would have afforded Rolls-Royce Limited. In short, Rolls-Royce would have dominated the high bypass aero-engine markets.

From such a technological perspective the political arguments favoured by Labour, which focused on production costs and the economic advantages of size, supposedly enjoyed by US companies, a position promoted by the Plowden Report, were fundamentally flawed. Therefore, it can be argued, where technological merits were not considered, the Wilson Labour government's economic arguments, which were used against the UK's aviation industry in general, were also flawed. The Labour government's argument relative to the UK's aviation industry concerned itself with immediate costs and spurious advantages of size. Yet instead of championing a UK policy that fully supported the long-term strategic view, as was clearly required for the UK aviation industry, and in such a tone and manner as was clearly emphasised at presidential level in the US, Labour chose to ignore the long-term implications of their short-term actions. Labour's prejudiced views of focusing on the short-term benefits associated with the immediate costs of the UK aviation industry were at best naïve, maybe myopic and at their very worst, they were treacherous.

To be fair, the US Pratt & Whitney and General Electric companies were able to produce a high by-pass aero-engine but the performances of their technologies fell short of what the market required, of what the Law demanded and of what Rolls-Royce was both historically and technically capable of supplying to the world's aviation markets. Rolls-Royce Limited was also capable of establishing new markets and its family of Advanced Technology Engines, comprising the RB.203, the RB.207 and the RB.211, were a generation ahead and would enable the UK company to leapfrog its US competitors. The ATE's integrated design and the variations of scale exemplified the company's application of its visionary policy towards the aircraft industry: 'As suppliers of engines to the aircraft industry throughout the world, the policy of the Company is to foresee the requirements of the industry as a whole and not to follow single-track development of specific engine types.' (R-R 1951)

A High Stakes Game

Historically, since the advent of the jet engine/gas turbine, Rolls-Royce had introduced drastic and major innovations which were constantly upping the ante in the high stakes game, as the US historian Newhouse identifies the commercial competition, played between the UK and US aero-engine manufacturers.

The Rolls-Royce Nene, in 1944, was designed from the outset to be the most powerful aero engine in the world and the first to produce 5,000 lbst. The Derwent V, a 0.855 scale Nene, powered the Gloster Meteor to a world speed record of 606 mph in November 1945.

The world's first turboprop to fly, in November 1945, was the Rolls-Royce Trent.

The world's first two-shaft aero-engine was the Rolls-Royce RB.39 Clyde, first run in August 1945. Eleven Clyde engines were built and successfully tested to a total of over 3,000 hours.

The Rolls-Royce Dart gas turbine-propeller aero-engine, on 16 July 1948, lifted the prototype Vickers Viscount into the air. The Viscount was the world's first gas turbine-powered airliner.

Peter Twiss piloted the Rolls-Royce Avon RA.28-powered Fairey FD.2 when this aircraft was the first to achieve over 1,000 mph. In the process of breaking the 1,000 mph barrier, Twiss established a new world speed record of 1,132 mph in March 1956.

The Rolls-Royce RB.80 Conway was first run in 1953, and in 1960 became the first bypass aero-engine to enter airline service. The second generation of bypass aero-engine was the RB.140/1 Medway, developed for the DH.121 and the AW.681.

The Rolls-Royce RB.141 was designed to give guaranteed thrust rating of 15,000 lbst for a dry weight of 3,560 lbs. The engine was the first of a family of optimized airline engines and its design drew on a synthesis of Rolls-Royce's best achievements:

> We know how to make engines of very high pressure ratio (Tyne). We know how to make engines with air-cooled turbine blading and very high top temperature (advanced military Avon). We know how to make a by-pass engine (Conway). No other company in the world combines this knowledge. Starting with a clean sheet of paper we can design the optimum powerplant for a high subsonic airliner which will surpass the best that any other firm in the world can achieve.

The development of the RB.141 Medway in turn would lead to the RB.178 two-shaft high bypass aero-engine project, which was initiated in 1961. In due course the RB.178 engine would lead to the third generation of high bypass power-plants and the RB.203 Trent, the world's first three-shaft high bypass ratio aero-engine.

The proof of concept RB.203 was the first three-shaft engine successfully running in December 1967. The Rolls-Royce RB.203 Advanced Technology Engine was the first of a family of innovative and superior performance engines, which would include the RB.207 for the Airbus A.300 and the RB.211 for the US wide-body. It is interesting to note that Lionel Haworth of Rolls-Royce initially designed a three-shaft engine, the RCA.3, in 1942.

The innovative RB.203 and RB.211 were Rolls-Royce's third generation of high bypass aero-engines and technologically the ATE high bypass aero-engines were years ahead of the developmental offerings from the US P&W and GE companies, who were still trying to master second generation bypass technologies.

Rolls-Royce RB.41 Nene.
(Author)

A Rolls-Royce RB.37 Derwent.
(Author)

Rolls-Royce RB.50 Trent.
(Author)

Rolls-Royce RB.39 Clyde. (Author)

Rolls-Royce RB.53 Dart. (Author)

The Fairey FD.2. (Author)

A Rolls-Royce Avon 200 series. (Author)

A Rolls-Royce RB.80 Conway. (Author)

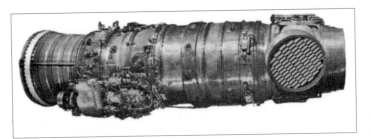

A RB.141 development engine. (Rolls-Royce)

Rolls-Royce ATE RB.211.
(Author)

Clearly, as one can appreciate when one reviews a history of Rolls-Royce's technical development in jet engines and gas turbines, the company's designers and engineers have repeatedly demonstrated their ability to provide innovative aero-engines and for those aero-engines to deliver the operating performance the designers intended and the operators required.

The Americans, too, have produced aero-engines but they have had to be guided in their initial efforts. However, rather than understand why the jet/gas turbine works, it seems the Americans would just accept that it did work and focused instead on trying to improve what there was. Through the employment of a reiterative style process, Pratt & Whitney's development of 'run em, bust em and fix em' efforts seemingly typified the US's aero-engineering strategy as solely focused on acquiring their technology through the development of established engines.

Monetizing Efforts

Seemingly, in the US, limitless amounts of money were thrown at engine performance issues and, with relatively little scientific forethought, the performance problems were literally 'trampled to death' under enormous monetizing efforts. This approach to fixing engineering problems was a relatively wasteful process and generated a huge escalation in related costs. Perhaps the significant escalation in costs, which began to be associated in the 1960s with the development of large jet engine and gas turbines, were directly attributable to the US style of problem solving; the costs passed on to the customer as the price of massively expanded yet crude and inefficient monetized development engineering effort.

It appears that knowledge can be acquired through a crude process of using massive resources to bludgeon a path of innovation through a monetized development process, and so provide a technology acquisition or acquisitions in a manner of speaking. Or, knowledge can be acquired through strategic vision and scientific processes, which are utilized to first establish theory, and then experiment proves the theory in support of the strategic vision.

Science and strategic vision were in abundance among the leading engineers in the UK during the 1940s and through to the 1960s. The situation in the US with massive development-led programs seems to suggest that enormous amounts of money would solve their problems, perhaps indicating a lack of or a failure to advance knowledge through other means.

Governments Determine

As an analogy of the competitive struggle between the US companies and Rolls-Royce during the establishment of the large high bypass ratio aero-engines, I would suggest that an organisation's learning curve advantages when financing or producing a bicycle count for little when your competitor is producing a car.

Technologically, Rolls-Royce was in a formidable position relative to General Electric and Pratt & Whitney, the only other industry players who were capable of playing catch up, if they were given the ball. However, it was left to the UK and US governments to determine whether Rolls-Royce would be allowed to commercially press home the UK company's advantageous position.

To achieve commercial success depends mainly on having technology that is better than the competition, but success also critically depends on being able to get the advanced technology to the market and to the customers who want to use it, in this case the commercial airlines. However, there existed complex external pressures which had to be taken into account by the Rolls-Royce company and the UK Labour government if they wanted the superior prime mover technology to succeed in the US, the world's largest and most lucrative commercial aviation market.

The pressures on the Rolls-Royce company, and its ATE family of engines, were part of a process that was engulfing the European aviation industry, which politically and commercially emanated from the USA. Hayward, in 1983, wrote of the process and the pressures that were in play during the late 1960s: 'The main pressure forcing the pace of this process was the need to match the scale of the American firms … European governments played a major role in the restructuring process…'

It is interesting to note that Armstrong-Siddeley, a UK-based company that was a relatively small player in US terms with a limited home market for its aero-engines, managed to sell its Sapphire aero-engine into the massive US military market. From 1950 onwards, the Sapphire, as the J65, was produced under license in the US by Curtiss-Wright and in massive quantities, some 13,000 overall. Despite the best US efforts to Americanize the engine, the US-produced engines which performed most effectively were those that followed the original British design. This observation of a British engine design powering the frontline defence of the USA sets in context the thrust and pace of the US politically-led economic changes, which would affect European defence and commercial aviation interests from the late 1950s and beyond.

A Faustian Pact

During the early 1960s, Rolls-Royce Limited had weathered the rationalisation and consolidation of the UK's aviation industry. The consolidation of the UK aviation industry was a political process which was carried out by both the Labour and Conservative governments and was conducted interdependently with US strategic aims. Despite the drastic changes which had occurred within the UK aviation industry in the late 1950s and early 1960s, Rolls-Royce had emerged as the UK and Europe's leading aero-engine company. As well as leading Europe's aero-engine companies, Rolls-Royce Limited was also the largest in terms of employment and among the top three aero-engine manufacturers in the world. Competing against the US aero-engine companies and their grand procurement plans, and their equally grand plans for financing the emerging HBR aero-engines, presented the commercially focused British company with a challenge: How to finance the ATE family in the face of grand US financial pressures.

Reflecting the new trends in US procurement processes, Rolls-Royce acknowledged that very large sums of money would be required for the project scoping, design, development and manufacturing of the medium and large sized ATE aero-engines. Most of the finance for the new aero-engines would have to be provided and used up-front in the design and development stages but because of the long term nature of jet engine projects, the initial low rate of return on investment would be not be commercially acceptable, therefore the normal lines of commercial finance would not be available. Such a position was nothing new to Rolls-Royce, as it was very much the nature of the business. In such circumstances Rolls-Royce had but one option – it would use the internationally recognised, industry-wide and legally acceptable method of government Launch Aid.

However, it seems that Rolls-Royce, notwithstanding the accommodation of Labour's political plan for the consolidation of the UK aerospace industry, which saw Rolls-Royce focus on the economic benefits and competitive advantages of scale, was part of a much larger and very complex trans-Atlantic view. In this view such key issues as intellectual property, technical advantage and commercial free trade were subjugated to political will. The politics affecting UK aviation policies at the time reflected the influence of UK and US interdependence and in such circumstances the political will of the UK would most probably have been subjected to 'normative transnationalism', an argument supported by Raj Roy and rejected by Henry Nau which states that economic interdependency impels political dependency. The economic power the US held over the UK would mean that the US impelled the UK's prescriptive politics.

Reflecting on these points, perhaps there is substance, contrary to Sandbrook's opinion, in what Ponting wrote when he claimed: 'Wilson sold his soul to Washington in a Faustian pact that saved Sterling while surrendering control of British policy.'

Trans-Atlantic Equations

Prior to the Second World War, the United States dominated the world's commercial aviation markets, which were powered by the US's prime mover piston engine technology. It was Sir Frank Whittle's invention of the jet/gas turbine aero-engine in the UK, together with its associated technologies, which caused the world-wide displacement of the piston engine in military and commercial aviation markets. After the Second World War, the jet engine became the new global prime mover, and the control of the technology was to have a major influence on the development of International politics and finance. (Pearson 1962)

The influence of the new prime mover technology would inform international politics and finance, in particular within the trans-Atlantic context, which would in turn set the legal and commercial framework for the much of the world's aviation industry. Arguably, had the initial trans-Atlantic equations established subsequent to the invention of the jet engine remained constant throughout the period, it is unlikely that the pressures identified by Hayward and which were later to be experienced by Rolls-Royce Limited would have been unequal. Arguably, with independent and due legal process, the pressures which were brought to bear on Rolls-Royce Limited could not have gathered sufficient momentum. Nor would the forces have been able to gain such traction that eventually they enabled those who controlled the pressures to cause the intended catastrophic consequence: the demise of Rolls-Royce Limited.

Politically, it seems that with the election of the Labour government in 1964, the UK aviation industry was doomed. This work uses evidence to highlight the case of Rolls-Royce, one of the most strategically important companies in the UK, which was to suffer the catastrophic consequences of the Labour government's political and economic interference. Thus interdependent political will and political strategy are probably the most important disablers or enablers affecting the commercial success or otherwise of the UK aviation industry and, significantly in this case, Rolls-Royce Limited.

It is asserted in this work that Rolls-Royce's design and development of its revolutionary three-shaft high by-pass ratio power-plant technologies, which would become focused solely on securing a position in the US market, provided the Wilson Labour government with a political opportunity. That opportunity would address Labour's determination to seek the demise of a large aircraft/aero-engine industry in the UK, provide much-needed technical assistance to the US and therefore present a set of circumstances conducive to obtaining a favourable US agreement for International Monetary Fund assistance to the UK.

This work revises the received view of Rolls-Royce as a poorly managed company that suffered from a typical British disease. Instead, drawing on the sources available, this work seeks to offer a politically credible and historically accurate counter view, one that portrays the turbulent events surrounding the collapse of Rolls-Royce Limited from a different perspective. This perspective shows that the blame lies squarely on the shoulders of the Labour government and the US administration.

As recent political and economic events are indicating, there seems to have been a repeat performance by the political left to undermine and over-reach certain companies and industries in the UK. The Lockheed/E.H.101 programme for the replacement of the US presidential flight is a probable candidate for investigation. Similar hallmarks appear to be stamped on the BAe Systems Nimrod M.R.4 and the Lockheed F-35 series of aircraft. Rolls-Royce, too, is facing its own repeat of history in a proposed version of an Anglo-US aero-engine for the Lockheed F35. The RR/GE engine has since been cancelled by the US administration and the jointly developed high technology programme's engines appear now to have fulfilled their function of accessing UK high technologies in advance of their application to a solely US-produced project. Should the distinguishing hallmarks of these programmes confirm the application of the political process of over-reach then the UK will be experiencing and witnessing the repeat of history. In so doing, we will have failed the security and economic welfare of our future generations because we will have failed to learn from the past mistakes.

The lessons of history are ours to learn from; they are with us now so that we may apply them for our futures. Therefore, the lessons provide us with the opportunity to avoid repeating the mistakes of the past.

CHAPTER ONE

BEING FIRST WITH A NEW TECHNOLOGY IS NOT ALWAYS AN ADVANTAGE

In the post-war era until the advent of the European Airbus, the United States dominated international aviation as a matter of policy. America forged its supremacy in Western aviation markets as a direct result of US policy, which stemmed from the post-Second World War Finletter report of 1948 that was commissioned by US President Truman.

In July 1947, President Truman, head of the United States, the most powerful country to emerge from the Second World War, which had aided the defeat of Nazi Germany and Imperial Japan, wrote:

> The rapid development of aviation in recent years has made many of our former concepts out of date. At the same time, there exists a danger that our national security may be jeopardized and our economic welfare diminished through a lowered aircraft production and a failure of the aircraft industry to keep abreast of modern methods, with consequent retarding of the development of air transportation. There is an urgent need at this time for an evaluation of the course which the United States should follow in order to obtain, for itself and the world the greatest possible benefits from aviation. (Finletter 1948)

The report clearly stated that the United States must obtain the new concepts which were then informing the rapid development of aviation. The US sought the leadership of the strategic technologies in an effort to secure the leading position over the US's international competitors to stave off the retardation of US air transportation. In particular, the 1948 report to the US president stressed the urgency with which the US had to better the UK in gas turbine technology and most importantly, in direct relation to the question of whether strategy or finance held greater importance, the report paid scant regard to the economist's cost-benefit analysis of achieving such a prospect. The development of the revolutionary prime mover technology in the United States was urgently prosecuted as a matter of prime importance:

> Power plants - The Commission has been advised by witnesses that gas turbines and rocket engines will ultimately replace reciprocating engines in future military aircraft. There is no doubt that these new and powerful power plants hold great promise for the

future and research and development on them must be pursued diligently. The jet engine is applicable to high speed fighters and fast bombers. It is the power plant that will make possible routine flights in the supersonic speed range. Its development, therefore, is of prime importance. (Finletter 1948)

According to Truman and his advisors, the United States was desperate to obtain a lead over the British in jet engine and gas turbine technology and then to claim the benefits for itself. A similar conclusion was arrived at in the Von Karman report that was presented, in July 1945, to Henry 'Hap' Arnold, Chief of Staff of the US Army Air Force. Von Karman singled out '… jet propulsion and jet powered aircraft …as the key future technologies…' (Hughes 1998) Despite the massive resources available to the USA, it was Great Britain which emerged from the war as the world leader in the jet/gas turbine aero-engine technologies.

As Sir Denning Pearson made clear in his review of the aero-engine industry of the West that he delivered in address to the Royal Aeronautical Society in 1962: 'At the end of the war, British industry was clearly ahead of the world in the development and production of gas turbine engines.'

Britain's commanding position in the radically innovative jet/gas turbine technology had been secured first by the lodging of patents and second by Frank Whittle's demonstration in being the first to operationally bench-prove his theories. Further evidence in support of Britain's superior technological position is advanced in Captain Eric Brown's book *Miles M.52*. Brown reveals that the Whittle W2/700, which was designed and produced to power Britain's supersonic aircraft, would incorporate afterburning and an aft-ducted fan. According to Brown the complete engine power-plant for the Miles M.52 was proving itself by July 1945 and supporting photographs of the engine on test are provided in his book. By way of comparison, the US Bell X-1, which the US would claim to have achieved the world's first supersonic flight, was powered by a rocket, as the advanced aero-engine technology was not within their reach.

Despite Corelli Barnett's contention that Britain's position as a world leader in post-Second World War aviation was taken for granted on the grounds of 'prestige', I suggest instead that there existed substantial grounds in design, development and the holding of intellectual property which gave Great Britain solid reasons to believe it had command over the disruptive jet/gas turbine propulsion technology. These substantial grounds were to be the primary drivers of aircraft design in the world's aviation industries in a post-piston-engined world. (Gunston. 1971)

As Newhouse sardonically recalled:

Having pioneered the jet engine during World War II, their [British] aim had been to exploit its advantages over piston engines and jump to a commanding lead over the Americans, who lagged behind in this technology.

The major industrial economies recognised the importance of the new prime mover technology and the significant influence it would exert on state policies. The new technology would drastically affect operations in critical areas such as defence projection, economic welfare and international communications. Whosoever would control the revolutionary technology would reap the immense political and financial prizes.

Give and Take

During the Second World War, Britain was favourably positioned to assist the Americans in deploying the new jet/gas turbine technology. The UK government had obtained the patents for jet/gas turbine aero-engine technologies, which had been developed by Whittle of the RAF and Power-Jets Limited, and by Griffiths, first while he was at the Royal Aircraft Establishment and then at Rolls-Royce Limited as Chief Scientist. A long-term and nationally co-ordinated strategic vision appears to have guided the UK's Ministry of Aircraft Production as it employed a policy of building on the UK's command of the new jet propulsion technology:

> When the Whittle bench test proved the potential success of jet propulsion, the Ministry of Aircraft Production put each British engine company to work on designs, so widening the possibilities of variation on the original basic patents. (Stevens 1953)

Prior to the culmination of hostilities and the close of the Second World War, the UK government and UK business interests sought to exploit the commercial advantages their command of the control of the revolutionary jet/gas turbine aero-engine technology would afford them. As Stroud confirms:

> During the 1939-45 war Britain became the leader in the development of the gas-turbine engine and when design began of the post war generation of transport aeroplanes the British aircraft industry was the first to exploit the turbine as a means of propulsion for commercial aircraft.

However, and as a condition of US help for the UK in its fight against the Nazis during the Second World War, in September 1941, Beaverbrook and Tizard had been instructed to grant the US the use of the initial jet/gas turbine aero-engine technology: 'For a total licence fee of $800,000 the USA was given full information on Whittle's various projects, and permission to use it for civil as well as military purposes.' (Gunston 2004)

Thus, where the wartime allies had shared technologies to aid the defeat of their common enemies, they were to be, ironically, peacetime antagonists in the battle for the establishment of the military and commercial gas turbine jet engine technology and the technology's economic development.

In 1942, the UK coalition government established the Brabazon Committee. In addition to considering developments in such areas as materials, aerofoils and manufacturing methods, the committee would also consider how best Britain's aviation industry might exploit its command of the new jet and gas turbine technologies. The Brabazon Committee sought to plan the development of strategic and commercial aircraft for the UK's own defence and commercial needs and to use the aircraft to gain financially in an effort to address the country's economic imbalances. A large part of the economic imbalance that Britain had been shackled with was the Morgenthau and White-inspired debt that was owed to the United States Treasury from the Second World War Lend-Lease agreement. Britain's strategic woes were America's business gains. As Skidelsky so aptly writes: 'The American reluctance to separate the business of business from the business of war was to become Britain's chief grievance against its wartime ally.'

A fuller picture of the anxious negotiations conducted between the UK and the US over the financial cost of Lend Lease and their economics *vis a vis* post war geo-politics is indicated by Skidelsky in his biography of John Maynard Keynes.

Washington, apparently unallied to moral complications, took full advantage of Whittle's engine, his plans and the Power-Jets engineers. Using their industrial and financial muscle, the US manufacturers had by 1944 managed to reach parity with the UK aero-engine companies in the power to weight ratio their aero-engines could produce. However, despite the scale of their industrial and financial advantages, the Americans fell behind their engineering competitors in the UK as Rolls-Royce quickly overtook them. Rolls-Royce's top jet-engine designers, led by Hooker and Lombard, produced the RB.40/41 Nene, a superior engine that delivered significant increases in performance over the competing US engines.

Turning Point

The jet engine designers and engineers at Rolls-Royce were prompted in their efforts by Hooker's visit to the US, where he witnessed the US attempts to take the lead. In response, Rolls-Royce designed and produced the Nene and despite the engine being, at the time, the world's most advanced and most powerful jet engine, the Nene's advantages were never fully exploited in the UK, and as a result the Nene engine never saw serious quantity production. In 1947, Rolls-Royce agreed to the license production of the Nene in the US, where Pratt & Whitney produced the engine in significant quantities as the P&W J42. Another significant event occurred in September 1946: at the express instance of Sir Stafford Cripps, a Labour Minister and left wing patent lawyer, Rolls-Royce was to supply its latest Nene and Derwent aero-engines to the USSR.

In the United States, the Rolls-Royce RB.41 Nene was known as the 'needle', ostensibly because it was used by the US government to needle the US gas turbine manufacturers into achieving a better engine performance than their British competitors. Another, but speculative, reason could quite possibly be because Cripps presented the Nene to the USSR, an engine that he decided was outdated technology, and that his action riled and needled the US administration. The testimony of the importance of the centrifugal jet engine technology to the Soviets is held up by the fact that over the years the USSR was to produce over 39,000 RD.45 engines, as the Nene was known in the Soviet Union, copied from the Rolls-Royce Nene and apparently free of all royalties due to the UK company. The Soviets also supplied the engine to China for which, it appears, they obtained a licence fee.

It is interesting to note that Cripps (Minister of Aircraft Production during the Second World War, President of the Board of Trade from August 1945 and then Chancellor of the Exchequer from November 1946) apparently thought to describe the centrifugal gas turbine technologies as outdated. Had Whittle's thermodynamic theories become obsolete by the time Cripps passed on Rolls-Royce's latest aero-engine technology to the USSR? The US aviation interests obviously did not think they were.

In February 1946, Sir Ben Lockspeiser, the Director General of Scientific Research MoAP, wrote in a note to F. G. Miles that the M.52 and the Whittle W.2/700 engine, for MoAP specification E.24/43, were to be discontinued. MoAP E.24/43 was the specification drawn up by the Ministry, in the autumn of 1943, when it was controlled by Cripps, for an aircraft that was to be capable of achieving 1,000 mph at 36,000 ft. Cripps chose the

Miles Aircraft Company to design and produce the aircraft and F. G. Miles, the company's chairman and managing director, was instructed to meet with Mr Lockspeiser, the then controller of research at the MoAP. The power plant for the Miles M.52 (E.24/43) was to have been Whittle's W.2/700, which had among its revolutionary features a ducted aft fan and provision for afterburning.

In the same period as the cancellation of the M.52 took place, Air Commodore Whittle resigned from Power-Jets on the grounds of disagreement with official policy. Cripps, it appears, was involved on at least two occasions where the UK's advantages in aviation technologies were discontinued and the technical aspects, such as the all-moving tail plane, ended up on foreign projects and were used for significant gain by Great Britain's industrial competitors.

Whatever Cripps' reasons were, they seem to appear uncertain and perhaps the economic historian B. W. E. Alford's investigation provides an insight on some of Cripps' motives. Although Cripps is perhaps a topic for another book, his decision to class the then latest aero-engine technologies as outdated was without a doubt misguided. For an intelligent gentleman to have committed such an action places him on a par with either the most 'naive' or the most treacherous of politicians ever.

In the same time frame, another equally important event occurred when Rolls-Royce designed and developed the RB.44 Tay (P&W J48) 'at the request of Pratt & Whitney'. This engine followed on from the RB.41 Nene and was the manifestation of the company's designers' complete mastery of the centrifugal turbojet technology. The result was an 'outstanding engine that combined all that was best in the technology of Whittle and Rolls-Royce'.

However, as Bill Gunston points out: 'This engine found no application except in licensed forms by Pratt & Whitney ... another failure by Britain to use a world beating engine.'

Were these historic events a turning point in the UK's post-war political and economic dealings with the new post-Second World War world order? It is perhaps at this point in the history of the jet and gas turbine in the UK where Gunston identifies that 'the rot had set in at the political level'.

A Whittle W2/700 on display at the MoSI, Manchester. (Author)

The Rolls-Royce
RB.41 Nene.
(Author)

The Co-Development of the Axial aero-engine

A limiting factor in the development of Whittle's centrifugal gas turbine technology is that engine performance is exponentially linked with size. This placed the centrifugal engine at a disadvantage to the axial gas turbine and efforts in all countries with access to axial compressor technology increased apace to develop axial jet engines. These efforts to gain the operational advantages afforded by axial technology were conducted to secure a position in the supply of axial jet technology and possibly as a way for nations to secure a means of avoiding the strategic limitations which would have been imposed by Britain's control of jet/gas turbine IPR patents.

After the close of the Second World War, German developments of jet/gas turbine aero-engine technologies were appropriated by the United States, the USSR and France. These efforts included advances in axial aero-engine compressor technologies, yet Great Britain's Griffiths and Whittle had already set the theoretical, and therefore the technical, precedents for all future jet/gas turbine aero-engines.

In the international race to develop axial technology, the initial advantages went to those countries whose industries had long experience of designing and producing steam turbine compressor technology. In the UK, work had commenced on axial compressor and gas turbine technology at the Royal Aircraft Establishment Farnborough and was, in 1926, stimulated by Dr A. A. Griffith's staff paper, entitled *An Aerodynamic Theory of Turbine Design*, on the axial flow gas turbine for aircraft propulsion.

Although a small axial compressor/turbine rig had been tested with encouraging results in 1929, work on gas turbines at RAE Farnborough lapsed until 1936, when Hayne Constant joined Griffith and Howell on his return to RAE from Imperial College. In 1938, the RAE placed an order with the Metropolitan-Vickers company (Metrovick) for the detail design, production and testing of the B.10 experimental axial flow compressor. The B.10 compressor was built and tested in December 1939 with encouraging results and the

Metrovick B.10.
(Author)

complete machine was run in an experimental test house at Trafford Park in December 1940.

In July 1940 the RAE handed over Hayne Constant's work on the F.1 design for an axial flow jet to Metrovick and by December 1941 the steam turbine department at Trafford Park began testing Britain's first axial flow jet engine: the F.2/1.

The F.2/1 was the first non-German axial jet engine in the world and the first application of the D.11's compressor developments. Further development of the F.2/1 saw useful increases in engine/compressor performance, which resulted in the engine being flight tested, in June 1943, in the tail of a modified Avro Lancaster. In November 1943, two Metrovick F.2s, each developing 1,800 lbst, powered the second prototype of the Gloster Meteor.

Metrovick's compressor was further developed in the F.2/4 Beryl (3,750 lbst) and was to eventually provide the heritage for Armstrong-Siddeley to build on in its design and production of the F.9 Sapphire (7,000 lbst) axial engine, an engine that at the time incorporated the world's most advanced compressor. The F.9 Sapphire advanced aero-dynamic compressor was designed by the chief engineer, Dr D. M. Smith, who contributed a significant step forward in aerodynamics and a step that gave the Sapphire aero-engine its superior operating performance. Whyte highlighted the outstanding aero-dynamic design of the compressor:

> Undoubtedly the most important main component contributing to the Sapphire's success is its 13 stage axial compressor. Its outstanding aerodynamic design is a heritage of its Metropolitan-Vickers origin, and its mechanical development is almost entirely owed to Armstrong-Siddeleys.

Armstrong-Siddeley took over Metrovick's gas turbine technology when, in 1947, the Manchester company was pushed by Ministry pressure to exit aviation. The engine was developed over time by Armstrong-Siddeley and under series manufacture the Sapphire was license-built in the US in enormous numbers as the Curtiss-Wright J.65.

A Rolls-Royce axial jet engine that was to share in the benefits of the outstanding aerodynamic design of the Metrovick compressor was the Avon. The Avon, under the Barnoldswick team led by Hooker, Lombard and H. Pearson among others, had started life as the (Axial Jet) AJ.65. Griffith's axial research, together with the work of Constant and A. R. Howell of the RAE, informed the axial compressor development work carried out by Rolls-Royce on the AJ.65. The eighth re-iteration of the AJ.65 gas turbine design would be developed by Rolls-Royce to incorporate Armstrong-Siddeley's compressor design knowledge, which was gained as a result of an exchange of information between the two companies.

This was unsurprising as both the Sapphire and Avon programmes were financed by the UK government. Reflecting the broad research approach the UK government took in the development of Whittle's patents, the UK government cast its net towards securing patent variations. The government invited the Halford and de Havilland, Bristol, Metrovick, Armstrong-Siddeley Motors, Napier and Rolls-Royce companies to become involved in the development of the jet/gas turbine because they were best positioned to develop the new technologies through their operating experience with aero-engine technologies, their scientific and their industrial capabilities.

With such a significant background in the development and production of axial gas turbine technology, the UK government wisely sought to exploit its intellectual property rights for commercial advantage. In the early stages of the jet/gas turbine aero-engine technologies, the UK government sought to map out the development and diffusion of the technologies and how their use in the new communications era would benefit and afford the world's major economies.

Politically, the control of the jet engine technology would allow Britain to continue to hold a world presence among the post-Second World War nations, as the control of the new technology would dictate the new frequencies of international communications. Economically, the new technology would grant Britain the right to decide who could afford to use the new gas turbine technology, how it would be used and where and when it would be used. The new gas turbine technology would mean that financially Britain stood to gain significantly by it.

However, and despite sustained British efforts following the end of the Second World War, for example by the Bristol and Rolls-Royce companies to crack the lucrative US domestic jet market, with jet engines incorporating more advanced technologies than were available in the contemporary US companies' jet engines, both Bristol and Rolls-Royce failed in their attempts. Yet, in 1968, utilizing a similar strategy of proposing the use of advanced technology on the ATE engine family to produce a range of engines of superior performance to those which their US competitors had to offer, witness Douglas, Fairchild and Lockheed, Rolls-Royce was to suddenly achieve a dramatic turnaround in fortunes. The US politically accepted the British company's aero-engines, to be used in quantity on a US airliner. Rolls-Royce secured a contract to supply its RB.211 to the US Lockheed Corporation to power the L1011 wide body airliner.

Metrovick F.2. (Author)

Metrovick F.2/4 Beryl. (Author)

Rolls-Royce Avon 1C. (Author)

The Metrovick-designed thirteen-stage compressor in an Armstrong Siddeley Sapphire. (Author)

The Rolls-Royce RB.211-powered Lockheed L1011 Tristar. (RAeS)

Revisiting the history of the Rolls-Royce RB.211

'Rolls-Royce's £150m US order climax to hard-fought campaign', exclaimed Kenneth Owen in *The Times* of 30 March 1968:

> When Rolls-Royce last night announced a £150m United States order for its RB211 turbo-fan engine – as part of the biggest civil aviation purchase ever made – Sir Denning Pearson, deputy chairman and chief executive, said: 'The outcome of this hard-fought sales campaign confirms the ability of a technologically based British industry to expand its penetration of the United States market.' (Owen, Kenneth, *The Times*, 30 March 1968, p. 11)

On 29 March 1968, Rolls-Royce aero engine division announced it had 'won the biggest single export order ever achieved by any section of British industry' with an order from Lockheed for the RB.211 to power the L1011 exclusively.

On 1 April 1968, Anthony Wedgwood Benn, the Minister of Technology in Wilson's Labour government, addressed Parliament:

> Hon. Members will already know that Rolls-Royce Ltd. has been successful in gaining a most valuable order in the United States to supply RB.211 advanced technology engines for the Lockheed Airbus. (Hansard 1968)

Anthony Wedgwood Benn was very proud of his government's interesting involvement in bringing about Rolls-Royce's success as his reply to Mr Maudling makes clear:

> Mr Maudling
> This is a great achievement by British industry. We on this side of the House would also like to pay our tribute to the company, to Sir Denning Pearson, Mr. Huddie and all the team who have achieved so much in this remarkable sale. Will the Minister stress, as I think he should, that this is an example of what British firms can do in selling in the American market, despite all that is often said about political difficulties? If people have quality, price and effort, they can sell on a very great scale.

> Mr Benn
> I am sure that the whole House would want to convey the congratulations given by the right hon. Gentleman, and it might also, on reflection, want to add that this is an interesting example of a partnership between Government and industry which has made this possible. I think that the right hon. Gentleman is a little less than generous in not making any reference whatsoever to that aspect.

Benn was congratulating himself and Rolls-Royce for securing the largest export order in British history. It remains to be seen whether and how much Benn also wanted to be held accountable for the collapse of Rolls-Royce Limited in 1971.

The order for British aero-engines was a significant event in aviation history, not only for its economic importance in that it helped to address the UK's extremely unhealthy balance of payments deficit but also, as *The Economist* on 6 April 1968 noted, because it significantly altered the structure of the industry: 'The [Rolls-Royce] result is a major,

A Rolls-Royce RB.211-22B. (Author)

structural change in the pattern of the world's aircraft industries.'

Peter Pugh, in *The Magic of a Name*, a three-volume history of Rolls-Royce, wrote: 'The British press went mad with delight.' Pugh quotes extensively from British press records with evidence from articles proclaiming the great success.

Bill Gunston, in his book *Rolls-Royce Aero Engines*, emphasised the technical and financial merits of the RB.211: 'In March 1968 Lockheed and its launch customers picked the Rolls-Royce engine, which technically and financially appeared too good to refuse.'

It is from such a standpoint in the received view that I shall not provide extensive coverage of the great success Rolls-Royce achieved in gaining the Lockheed L1011 contract for the RB.211, as it is already very well covered in British history, perhaps with the exceptions of Marr and Sandbrook. However the events in Rolls-Royce's history are viewed, it is important that the deal between Lockheed and Rolls-Royce is firmly etched on this great country's political and industrial consciences as there are significant historical lessons to be learned.

In the US, at NASA, they too acknowledge the historical significance of the British Rolls-Royce RB.211 engine, although it is couched in their language and on their terms:

At the outset, Lockheed's engineers knew that they needed a short engine to fit this installation. Neither General Electric nor Pratt & Whitney had what they wanted, but a third player was at hand: Britain's Rolls-Royce. That company had a design on paper for a new engine, the RB-211, along with a very aggressive head of its Aero Engine Department, David Huddie.

However, as is clearly indicated by the language that Heppenheimer and Dick use in their US version of events, the Americans looked on Rolls-Royce as a 'third player'. 'Rolls', they emphasise, 'had never cracked the domestic market in America, the world's most lucrative…'

It is at this point that I wish to draw the reader's attention to a number of anomalies I am associating with the received view of the RB.211 history, the view that has been portrayed publicly, namely:

First: The signing of the Lockheed order by Rolls-Royce came almost a month after American Airlines was to announce to the American press that it had ordered DC-10 aircraft with Rolls-Royce RB.211 engines.

Second: Rolls-Royce signed a contract with Lockheed for the RB.211-06 version and almost as soon as the ink had dried on the signatures, Lockheed informed the British company that it would have to significantly change the engine's design and performance specifications to the RB.211-22 at no extra cost to the US company.

Third: Lockheed brought forward its requirements for increased engine thrust by two years, putting additional pressure on Rolls-Royce, and the increased costs were to be borne by the UK company. Overall, Lockheed's requirements for additional thrust would increase the RB.211 initial thrust design from 33,260 lbst (1967) to over 41,000 lbst (1971).

Fourth: Despite neither of the US companies having the technology to address Lockheed's needs, Lockheed insisted that Rolls-Royce provide an extremely competitive price in relation to the Pratt & Whitney and General Electric products.

Fifth: The open contract scenario, which Rolls-Royce seemed to have accepted, as indicated by the finalisation of the design changes requested by Lockheed being somewhere towards the latter part of 1968, was almost from the start impossible, but nevertheless the flexibility of the initial contract was fully supported by the UK Labour government and its Minister of Technology. Rolls-Royce's original forecasts, time, material and costs, had been based on the development of the original RB.211 06/10 aero-engine series. These project estimates were used to inform the Labour government in its discussions with Rolls-Royce's application for launch aid. The major re-specification by the customer of the engine design and performance, and the revised attendant costs, times and materials were not, it appears, reflected in an increased level of Labour government support, which from the start had set an upper limit on UK Launch Aid of £47 million.

Sixth: Rohr Industries, the US company responsible for building and supplying nacelles and pods for the Lockheed C5A and the Boeing 747, was known to be in talks with the Labour government's Minister of Technology from early 1968 with a view to trading Short Brothers. Shorts was the company, majority owned by the UK government, that Rolls-Royce had contracted to supply the RB.211's inlet ring and nacelle.

Seventh: Despite sustained efforts since the end of the Second World War by Rolls-Royce to crack the lucrative US domestic jet market, with jet engines incorporating greater and more advanced technology than was available to the US jet engine companies, Rolls-Royce failed in its attempts. Yet, in 1968, utilizing a similar strategy of proposing the use of advanced technology on the ATE engine family to produce a range of engines of superior performance to those which the US companies had to offer, witness Douglas, Fairchild and Lockheed, Rolls-Royce suddenly achieved a dramatic turnaround in fortunes with the US's political acceptance for its aero-engine to be used in quantity on a US airliner.

Eighth: Rolls-Royce, encouraged by industrial and political forces on both sides of the Atlantic, was developing a family of Advance Technology Engines (ATE) based on its innovative three shaft technology: the RB.203, the RB.207 and the RB.211. Subsequent to the US's political acceptance of the British RB.211 aero-engine being used on the Lockheed L1011, the RB.203 engine for a small-capacity short haul US Fairchild F-228 feeder-liner was cancelled, as was the RB.207 for the European A.300 Airbus. Only the RB.211 engine from the projected family survived. In a similar time frame, the US government funded research to review three-shaft engine technologies and this was initiated and coincided with the demise of the RB.203-powered US Fairchild F228.

Ninth: Rolls-Royce from the outset designed its ATE family to be supplied to the US wide-body and feeder-liner airliner markets as a totally integrated propulsion package. That the engine together with its nacelle and pod would be engineered as one was a unique feature of the Rolls-Royce three-shaft ATE aero-engine family, and a technical position that was not mirrored by either GE or P&W. The total cost to the UK government of developing the ATE RB.211 was to include the complete power-plant package, whereas the GE and P&W had developed their initial engines on the back of a US government/DoD contract. In both cases, the US engines were supplied bare and not as part of an integral power-plant, nor did either GE or P&W accept responsibility for their respective engines' installed performance on the aircraft.

Tenth: Hawker Siddeley Aviation together with Rolls-Royce, and previously Bristol Siddeley, worked more closely than was usual in the aircraft industry to produce an engine, nacelle, pod and pylon combination that was scientifically and aero-dynamically best matched to Hawker Siddeley's new aft loaded wing that was then in the process of being designed and developed for the Airbus A.300.

Eleventh: General Electric has been credited, in the received view, with being more advanced in achieving higher Turbine Entry Temperatures (1,377°C) on its TF.39 high by-pass turbofan programme than Rolls-Royce was able to achieve in its development of TETs for the RB.211. Yet one of the benefits of Rolls-Royce's takeover of Bristol Siddeley Engines in 1966 was access to the high Turbine Entry Temperature technology employed on Concorde's Olympus 593 engines, which were designed to operate with a design TET in the region of 1,450°C.

This list of anomalies are by no means exhaustive, nor are the positions of the points of interest to the author an indication of their importance – all of them are equally important. Critical for this study is the fact that few, if any, references are made to any or all of the points of interest and it is for this reason that the author has investigated a little further to see why these points have not been addressed by historians of whatever persuasion, and how history might look if they were included in an established received view.

CHAPTER TWO

LOCATING THE POWER

Technology, Politics and Commerce

It is a little known fact that in February 1968, a little over a month before Rolls-Royce Limited signed a contract with Lockheed on 29 March for the supply of the RB.211 on the L-1011, American Airlines on 19 February 1968 announced that it had ordered the McDonnell Douglas DC-10. By 29 February, the American Airlines order seemed destined to be powered by Rolls-Royce RB.211 engines. Curiously, in March 1968, an American Airlines press conference confirming the Rolls-Royce order was cancelled at the last minute and so too was the combination of the DC-10 aircraft and RB.211 engine.

Why was the American Airlines order for the RB.211-powered DC-10 cancelled at the last minute? What were the reasons given for the cancellation of the Rolls-Royce RB.211 order for the American DC-10? Do the two align? Curiously, historians of aviation, generally, do not engage with this issue.

The Pressures to Build Anew

A new era of US mass air transport opened when on 19 February 1968, American Airlines announced it had selected the new large capacity McDonnell Douglas DC-10 airliner as its US air bus.

The wide-body McDonnell Douglas DC-10 aircraft was representative of the innovative aircraft and aero-engine technologies which were then being adopted by US and European airframe manufacturers to provide airlines with aircraft of very large carrying capacity and short/medium to long range.

As well as McDonnell Douglas, other airframe manufacturers who were to produce aircraft for similar markets were Boeing with its 747, Lockheed with its L1011 and Airbus with the A.300B. These very large capacity aircraft were needed to address the significant increases in passenger numbers and air traffic which were then being forecast by the industry. The forecasts were based on the continuing upward commercial trends in passenger traffic which were then being experienced by airlines in general. Historically the commercial airline trends, which were being driven by engine technology developments, were influenced by social and economic factors and these informed US economic planning and regulatory responses.

The first of the US air buses. The DC-10 takes off for its maiden flight on 29 August 1970. (RAeS)

When one considers the drastic impact the development of the jet turbine had on the US economy, one can understand it was of immense proportions and the size of the impact underlined the significant influence of aviation on political and economic thinking in the US. In relation, for the US to lose technological control of the development of the aviation power-plant to a foreign nation, like Britain, was unthinkable as it would mean losing control of the powerful forces governing the standards of speed, safety, regularity, comfort and economy; it would mean the US giving up their independence. Losing control, to summarize Truman, would jeopardize US national security and diminish US economic welfare.

Changing the Game

In Europe, large capacity airliner concept studies had been carried out by both private and government organisations since the late 1950s and early 1960s. The studies in Europe had been conducted by Hawker Siddeley Aviation, Nord-Aviation, Breguet, the British Aircraft Corporation and SUD-Aviation. These aviation companies considered the airline industry's needs for suitable aircraft designs in the new large capacity and short to medium range sectors. In 1964, the UK government Royal Aircraft Establishment-led Lighthill Committee also looked into the matter of a future short haul, high capacity commercial aircraft. 'Initial studies of high capacity short-haul ... date back to the Lighthill Committee of 1964.'

Many of the studies conducted by the aviation companies were weighted towards a 200 to 300 seat aircraft, with a high cycle performance that was based on the utilization of the game-changing new technology of the high by-pass ratio aero-engine. In the UK, Hawker Siddeley Aviation, following on from its experience with the DH.121/Trident, proposed two new designs for BEA which were based on the concept of using two of the large High Bypass Ratio engines to enhance aircraft performance.

Between 1964 and 1967, Hawker Siddeley Aviation's examination of BEA's requirements produced the 160-seat HS.132 and the 185-seat HS.134; both offered the prospect of a 25–30 per cent reduction in seat mile costs over aircraft then in service. Both of the designs would have utilized two of the new technology Rolls-Royce RB.178 HBR aero-engines of 30,000 lbst to provide superior operating performance over their first generation three-engine contemporaries, and paved the way for later work on the Airbus.

Designs using two large engines had their advantages. One of the main points that emerged was that, due to having to cater for the engine out condition, a high power-to-weight ratio resulted. This gave high rates of climb, reducing both block times and community noise levels.

In March 1966, under the aegis of an Anglo-French Ministry working party an *Outline Specification for a High Capacity Short Haul Aircraft* was issued. Hawker Siddeley, together with Nord and Breguet, proposed the large twin engine HBN.100, a design that amply met the government-prepared specification. Powered by two Rolls-Royce RB.178 aero-engines or two equivalent American Pratt & Whitney JT9Ds, the designs projected a 30 per cent reduction in direct operating costs compared to its three engine contemporaries.

In France, SUD-Aviation was projecting the Galion, so named to emphasise the return to Europe of the riches of the Americas. The Galion was to have been powered by either the Rolls-Royce RB.178-14 or an Anglo-French joint Bristol Siddeley/SNECMA BS.123-03 high by-pass ratio turbofan.

Quite clearly, the Eurocentric designs addressed shared European political and commercial imperatives and importantly, the aircraft designs they projected would compete in the European home and world markets. By comparison, the US aircraft project studies of the time followed the Europeans' lead. For example, Lockheed's initial twin L-1011 reaffirmed US intentions towards Europe's aviation industry, by taking the European twin large capacity air bus and adopting it as their own. Lockheed's designs for a US wide-body were reactions to the designs then being considered in Europe, and as such sought to maintain and extend the US's domination and colonization of Europe through the skies.

Locating the Knowledge

The critical technological element that enabled aircraft designers to pursue larger capacity jet powered aircraft was the High By-pass Ratio (HBR) technology ducted fan aero-engine. Sir Frank Whittle, on 4 March 1936, originally filed an application for patenting his thrust augmenter. The Complete Specification was accepted on September 3 1937, as UK patent No. 471,368.

Sir Frank Whittle explained the reasoning for his 'bypass engine':

From the earliest days, I had been seeking a means of improving the propulsive efficiency of jet engines. I had always realized that it was desirable to 'gear down' the jet, i.e., to generate a high mass low velocity jet rather than a low mass high velocity jet of the straight jet engine. To this end, I filed a patent application in 1936 for what we then called a 'bypass engine' but later came to be known as the turbofan. (Boyne and Lopez 1979)

Subsequently Whittle's bypass engine became known as the augmenter, or the ducted fan or the turbofan, and the technology was further developed under separate initiatives by Rolls-Royce in the UK and by the General Electric and Pratt & Whitney corporations in the US.

Although Whittle was to learn that Dr Harris of Esher had patented the concept for a ducted fan in 1917, Whittle's 1936 patent is officially and internationally acknowledged as having established the thermodynamic principles for all subsequent turbofan, ducted fan and by-pass aero-engines.

The Principle Theory of By-Pass

A former Technical Director of Rolls-Royce Plc explained the reason and origin of the by-pass: '[Whittle's 1936 patent]… embodied the thermodynamic principles of all subsequent by-pass engines.'

Professor Riti Singh, in his 2001 Chairman's address to the aerospace industries acknowledged the enormous achievements attributable to the invention, innovations and the development of the gas turbine, which were first embodied in Whittle's works:

> The magnitude of Whittle's achievement can be perhaps appreciated by recognizing that the world's three major 'Prime manufacturers' of gas turbines, namely Rolls-Royce, Pratt and Whitney and General Electric all started their gas turbine business based on Whittle's W2/700 gas turbine.

Despite being popularly associated with the centrifugal compressor, Whittle's first patent clearly indicated he was fully aware of the advantages offered by an axial compressor engine. He also fully appreciated the efficiency advantages of the bypass engine over the pure jet, yet it was to be over twenty years before commercial aviation was to benefit from his work. Unfortunately for Whittle, his bypass/thrust augmenter patent expired in 1962 just as turbofans became fashionable.

In Brown's article 'The Origin of the Bypass and Ducted Fan', published in *The Aeroplane* on 13 March 1959, Brown drew attention to the technology's lack of commercial use and offered plausible reasons as to why the bypass had not been taken up and put into service. Yet, despite the offered reasons, Mr Justice Lloyd-Jacob remarked on the technology's distinct lack of commercial application:

> The history of the non-exploitation of the invention after its publication, as deposed to in the evidence before me, is one of almost unrelieved frustration, and the recital by Sir Frank Whittle of his unavailing attempts to awake interest in the bypass engine made melancholy hearing.

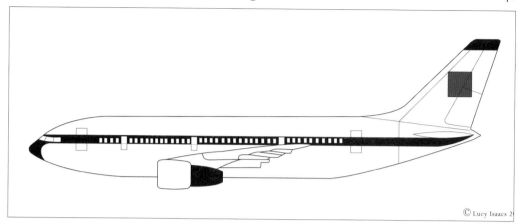

HBN.100. (Lucy Isaacs)

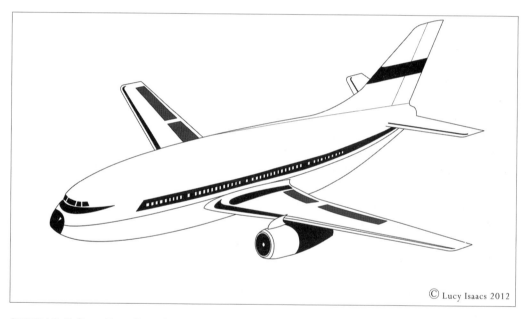

SUD/BAC Galion. (Lucy Isaacs)

Sir Frank Whittle.

Early attempts were made to prove the bypass concept with engines such as the Griffiths C.R.1, 1940 (bpr 7:1); and the C.R.2, 1944 (bpr 2:1). The Metrovick F.3 ducted aft fan, in 1943, was to provide a significant performance insight into the scale of efficiency a bypass engine was to offer over a turbojet. PowerJets also developed the Whittle W2/700 with aft-ducted fan and afterburning to power the Miles M.52. Later still, both Rolls-Royce and General Electric produced Aft Fan engines, but despite these early attempts, the distinct engine performance and economic advantages which the bypass technology offered the airlines were not fully considered for commercial exploitation until the early 1960s.

In the early 1960s, coinciding with the expiration of Whittle's patent, the US General Electric and Pratt & Whitney aero-engine companies jumped at the opportunity to use the ducted fan and high bypass technologies, which the Americans refer to as the turbofan. In 1962, the same year that Whittle's ducted fan patent expired, the US Department of Defense financed the initiation of the development of high bypass ratio turbofan technology for use on the USAF CX-HLS project. The USAF CX-HLS project would eventually become known as the Lockheed C5A, a high capacity and long range strategic transport aircraft.

In the UK, Rolls-Royce dusted off its early large bypass engine plans and with the benefit of over twenty years of bypass design and development experience behind it, the company made known its interest in the emerging large capacity market, determined not to let the Americans steal a march. Rolls-Royce, anticipating the changes, had actually started to plan for the development of the RB.178 large high by-pass aero-engine back in 1960, when it recognized at an early stage in the Conway's commercial life that the airlines would need more power to counter the colonization from the skies.

In Europe and the United States, national and international programmes were initiated in an attempt to gain leverage towards achieving the competitive advantages of a first mover. Being first, technically, could secure commercial riches and powerful political advantages. These would stem from and be afforded to the first nation or nations to produce an aircraft that efficiently addressed the requirements of the agreed Bermudian defined markets. Thus, the stage was set for either collaboration or confrontation between the respective nations, their industries and their competing technologies.

From this brief observation on the introduction of the bypass and ducted fan technology to power emerging markets, it is patently clear that there existed commercial obstructions and political inhibitors which delayed the advanced technology from reaching its full potential at a much earlier point in time. Also clear, once the patent expired, were the political and military driving forces behind the adoption of the revolutionary jet aero-engine technology. It is apparent that the bypass/turbofan technologies were prioritized at multiple political, technological, commercial and industrial levels.

The McDonnell Douglas DC-10

One of the first of the new large capacity commercial aircraft to utilize the revolutionary bypass aero-engine technology, which stemmed directly from Whittle's 1936 patent, was the McDonnell-Douglas DC-10.

The Whittle
W2/700. (Author)

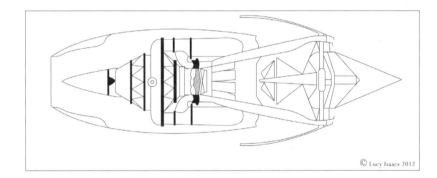

Whittle Aft Fan.
(Lucy Isaacs)

The C.R.1.,
Griffiths'
Rolls-Royce
counter rotating
experimental
compressor for a
7 bpr ducted fan.
(Author)

On 29 August 1970, the latest Douglas airliner, the DC-10, the first from the newly created McDonnell-Douglas Corporation, lifted off on its maiden flight. The moment was the culmination of technical innovation, of political intrigue and economic sparring which stretches back in the history of aviation.

The commercial Douglas DC-10 started life as a project that drew heavily on the Douglas company's bid, in 1965, for the CX-HLS, the USAF's very large strategic transport aircraft project. Various designs for a very large aircraft powered by four of the newly projected high by-pass turbofan engines were considered by the Douglas designers before that company became part of McDonnell-Douglas in 1966.

American's Jumbo Twin

In April 1966, Franklin Kolk, American Airlines' chief engineer, held a meeting at Lockheed Burbank where he outlined his requirement for a specific twin-engine, air bus-type aircraft to fulfil his airline's future short range, large capacity needs. 'From Burbank, Kolk flew on to call on Douglas, which was also interested.' Kolk was convinced of the significant operating cost reductions a twin high by-pass turbofan engine, high cycle and high capacity air bus type aircraft would bring to American Airlines. In US aviation lore, Kolk had initiated the 'Jumbo Twin' and later, the revolutionary specification set by American Airlines' chief engineer would become known as the Kolk machine.

Kolk's actions were in response to Boeing and Pan American's designs for the new large capacity sectors. Un-impressed with what he perceived as Juan Trippe and Bill Allen's manipulation of the civil jet market and their newly announced 747, Frank Kolk called for an aircraft with a capacity that was mid-way between the DC8/707 and the 747, an aircraft specification similar to what the Europeans were referring to as an air bus.

A Pinch of SALT

According to Newhouse, the author of the US history of the Strategic Arms Limitation Talks, there was no connection in timing between Kolk's aircraft specification and the Boeing 747. Newhouse wrote that the timing of the two projects was pure coincidence. In contrast to Newhouse, the US aviation historian Heppenheimer (1995) presents Kolk's reasoning for American Airlines' preference for an alternative aircraft to the Pan-Am/Boeing 747: 'Kolk's attitude was that it was high time to put an end to Trippe's habit of coercing the domestic airlines into buying equipment they didn't need and could barely afford.'

I suggest Kolk, as American Airlines' chief engineer, had the foresight and the authority to promote his vision and drive forward significant changes within the US airline industry. The success of American Airlines, to a very high degree, relied upon the aircraft they flew, and Kolk as the chief engineer and C. R. Smith as the president determined which aircraft American Airlines bought and operated.

Kolk and Smith had challenged the US industry before when on 17 July 1963 they ordered the BAC 1-11, a British aircraft powered by Rolls-Royce engines. They signed a

Metrovick F2 nine-stage
compressor and F3 aft
fan. (Author)

Rolls-Royce Avon with aft
fan. (Author)

contract to import the British aircraft because at the time of their negotiations with BAC, the similar Douglas DC-9 was not then available from the US manufacturer, and American Airlines would not be forced into taking something that was not suited to their business.

Finding themselves in a similar situation, with the prospect of being coerced to take the Pan-Am/Boeing/P&W offering, Kolk and Smith drew up a technical specification for an aircraft that addressed American's business needs and which shared similar technologies to those which featured on European designs for a twin-engine, short haul, large capacity air bus. From a historical perspective, it appears that American Airlines was well positioned, technically and commercially, and had the political experience to bypass the US Civil Aeronautics Board and carry through the acquisition of a foreign European twin-engine aircraft powered by foreign British high by-pass ratio engines.

In the US, the Douglas company responded to Kolk's Jumbo Twin request. On 19 May 1966, *Flight* reported that Mr Jackson R. McGowen, Douglas group vice-president, aircraft, had revealed plans for a short haul, twin-engined 250–350 seater which could be in service by late 1970 or early 1971. The new generation Douglas twin would have seriously challenged the noisy and fuel thirsty Boeing 727.

CHAPTER THREE

THE ORIGINS OF THE ROLLS-ROYCE HIGH BYPASS ENGINE

The technology that allowed Kolk to propose a large capacity twin-engine aircraft was similar to Rolls-Royce's projected high by-pass ratio turbofan, the RB.178, as proposed for the Boeing 747 and the H.B.N.100, an initial European air bus design. Rolls-Royce described the RB.178 aero-engine as the replacement for the R.Co. Conway, the world's first ducted by-pass aero-engine to see service.

The First Bypass Aero-Engine in Service: The Conway

The Rolls-Royce Conway utilized Whittle's thermodynamic principles, as indicated in the Power Jets L.R.1. The advanced twin shaft Conway engine, designed by Fred Morley from an idea promoted by Dr A. A. Griffiths, revolutionized commercial jet aircraft transport, outclassing in economics and engine performance the US competition's lesser efficient turbojets.

The roots of the Rolls-Royce Conway bypass engine go back to 1946 and a UK Air Ministry specification, B.35/46, which was similar in projected performance to the Power Jets L.R.1 project, an advanced ducted fan aero-engine that was cancelled by the UK Air Ministry in 1944:

[In 1946] Rolls-Royce became interested in the bypass formula as a result of the Air Ministry B.35/46 specification for the V-bombers. The terms of this included M0.87 cruise at 50,000ft over a range of 2,450 to 4,000nm. From the BJ.80 of February 1947 has been evolved the Conway … (Lombard 1960)

The RB.80 by-pass, or double-flow Conway design, was started in January 1950 and the engine first ran in August 1952. Although the engine's bypass ratio was relatively low at 0.23, the bypass airflow had a very high pressure ratio since it was compressed, or boosted, by all seven low pressure stages. The Conway R.Co 2 engine with the thrust rating of 9,250 lb was first flown in 1954, in a Rolls-Royce pod that carried the bypass airflow to the rear of the engine.

The carrying of the bypass airflow to the rear employed a concept utilized by A. A. Griffiths in the design of the C.R.2.

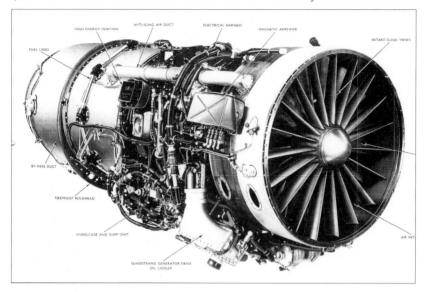

The Conway
by-pass engine.
(Rolls-Royce)

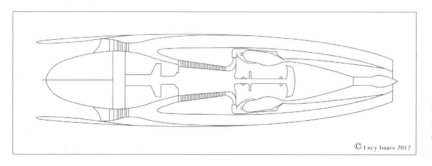

Power Jets L.R.1
ducted fan aero
engine, 1944.
(Lucy Isaacs)

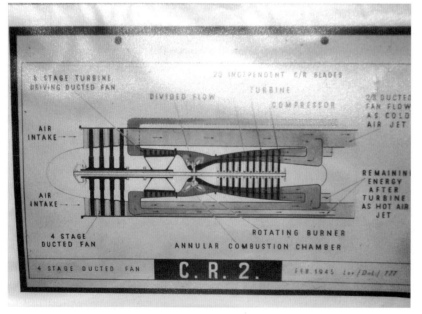

A. A. Griffiths'
C.R.2 design
for a four-stage
ducted fan dated
February 1945.
(Author)

Armstrong
Siddeley axial
turbojet ASX.
(Author)

The Griffiths C.R.2 was projected to compress air at the intake through a four-stage fan which was then fed into cold and hot jets. The cold efflux would represent two thirds of the intake and the remaining third would be compressed by a counter rotating compressor before exiting into an annular rotating combustor. The hot air from the multi-directional combustor would lead forward into a five-stage turbine driving the four-stage ducted fan as well as leading aft through the counter rotating turbines driving the high pressure compressor. Even earlier than the C.R.2 was the design for the C.R.1 bypass engine: 'Dating from 1940, this was a typically ingenious turbofan of bypass ratio 7...' (Gunston 1989)

Rolls-Royce built Griffiths' experimental C.R.1 fourteen-stage high pressure compressor and the unit went on test on 3 March 1942. The complexity of the fourteen-disc, double-deck turbo/compressor resulted in mass leakages and the project was abandoned in favour of the C.R.2.

The Case for the Gas Turbine

Whittle, in his paper 'The Case for the Gas Turbine', had identified the drag that was caused by the increase of air velocity over the surfaces forward of the propelling nozzle. To counter and offset the effects of the surface drag, Whittle proposed the use of a nozzle cowl. Rolls-Royce's use of a full-length bypass duct, a feature of the Whittle Power Jets L.R.1 design dating from 1944, would attend to the engine performance losses and improve, in theory, the specific fuel consumption.

The Conway incorporated many innovative features, such as a full-length bypass duct, which were to give the advanced aero-engine a significant operating edge over the American competition. The engine's importance for British aviation was, in 1953, emphasised by Sir George Edwards: 'The Conway is the most dramatic engine development since the war. It

Rolls-Royce
RB.80. A
Conway Mk
103. (Author)

shows such promise that it may well see everything else off on the North Atlantic run ten years from now.'

By 1953, the Rolls-Royce Conway by-pass aero-engine had been selected to power the Vickers-Armstrong V.1000 strategic transport for the RAF. The Rolls-Royce aero-engine had also been chosen to power the 150-seat Vickers commercial VC-7 trans-Atlantic airliner and the VC.7 was subsequently ordered by BOAC. By 1955 the very promising advanced technology R.Co 5 aero-engine had been type-tested at 13,000 lb thrust and was receiving priority backing from the UK government.

The Conway was proving itself as a significant technological achievement. The engine was meeting the performance expectations which informed the UK Air Ministry specification B.35/46. This further indicates that there existed a close alignment between the formulated expectations of the UK Air Ministry and the projected technological capabilities of Rolls-Royce's aero engineers and designers. The British government, through its various agencies such as the RAE, was in a position to fully understand the UK aviation industry's manufacturing capabilities and its technical aspirations.

A Sovereign Strategy for Technology Acquisition

Before the US had decided it had a need to be able to place US military assets anywhere in the western world, which would require a jet-powered strategic airlift capacity, the British were in the process of building a jet-powered long range large capacity aircraft.

The Vickers V.1000 was designed to support British military power by accompanying the V-Bombers anywhere in the British Empire; the Vickers V.1000 would fly further, faster and with greater capacity then any jet-powered transport before it or projected at the time.

Now the makers of the Viscount announce the Vickers 1000 military transport and V.C.7 civil variant. The aircraft ... has a span of 140ft, length 146ft and a height of fin 38ft 6in. Its seating capacity is variable between 100 and 150 seats, and the aircraft will be capable, by virtue of the economy of its Conways, of flying the longest intercontinental routes or of operating efficiently on comparatively short continental services; economical range flexibility for such duties may be between limits of about 400 and 4,000 miles.

One of the benefits envisaged by Vickers was that the technology developed for use in the military transport aircraft would be read across into a commercial version. 'Vickers was delighted that at long last it seemed possible to develop concurrently a military transport for the RAF and a commercial airliner for BOAC.' For the North Atlantic route, the aircraft was given six abreast seating and 'the wing was made slightly over generous to allow for maximum fuel'.

Drawing on their Valiant V-Bomber experience, the Vickers team at Weybridge were constructing the V.1000 prototype and had almost completed the airframe. The Vickers commercial airliner version, the VC-7, with a fuselage length of 137 ft 11 in and a diameter of 12 ft 4 in, was shown to prospective airlines around the world and drew favourable support even in the face of strong US activity supporting the early designs of the competing Boeing 707 and Douglas DC-8. Significantly, the US aircraft manufacturer Boeing, which was supplying the military version of the 707 as the KC-135 air tanker to the USAF, eventually responded to the international airlines' criticisms of the inadequate early 707 design.

Remarkably, because it is one of the costliest modifications a company can make, Boeing decided to increase the width as well as the length of the fuselage in the commercial 707, of which 20 were ordered by Pan Am on 13 October 1955. (Gunston)

In response to the Vickers VC-7, Boeing increased the length of its 707, from the prototype's 122 ft 2 in to 138 ft 10 in, and also increased the aircraft's width by 16 inches to 12 ft 4 in. (Janes 1966) The criticisms of Boeing's initial 707 from the international airlines, which Boeing hoped to sell the 707 to, prompted the inexperienced Boeing to change the 707's performance specification and capacity to something akin to what the airlines could expect from the superior Vickers VC-7.

As a measure of which aircraft design was more likely to be successful, an overview of the post-war commercial activities of Boeing and Vickers provides an interesting comparison. Whereas Vickers was successfully selling the Rolls-Royce Dart gas turbine-powered Viscount all over the world and doing so particularly well in the USA, Boeing could only offer up piston-engined aircraft in the post-war period. All three of Boeing's airliners were commercial failures: the Boeing 307 sold only ten, the 314 was a short production run and another poor performer was the Boeing 377 Stratocruiser, an airliner that was based on the B29 bomber. The piston-engined 377 Stratocruiser was produced between 1947 and 1949, sold only fifty-five and inflicted a loss of $15 million on the Boeing company.

Vickers was eventually to sell and deliver 444 Viscounts, indicating quite clearly in this instance that the UK aircraft manufacturer had correctly gauged the needs of the airlines. Whereas in Boeing's case, despite having the massive resources necessary to have built thousands of bombers for the USAF, it did not have what it took to cut it with the commercial airlines. In the immediate post-war period, the Boeing company had clearly lost to Vickers in the commercial world.

Yet surprisingly, just months short of the scheduled first flight, the Vickers V.1000 project was cancelled by the UK government MoS when, on 11 November 1955, the UK Treasury withdrew funding for the aircraft. British Overseas Airways Corporation (BOAC), the UK government-controlled and financed airline that flew the Atlantic between the UK and the US, had ordered the V.C.7 aircraft to operate on the trans-Atlantic route. Suddenly, the UK government-owned airline changed its mind and said that it had no interest in acquiring the Vickers V.C.7 aircraft and BOAC cancelled its order. However, a year later and with no equivalent British aircraft available, the blundering BOAC ordered the foreign Boeing 707 so that the British airline might compete with Pan American on the trans-Atlantic route. Of course, the British airline had to seek and be granted government approval before it could commit to the Boeing 707 order. Sir George Edwards, who was chief engineer for the Vickers V.1000/VC-7 programme, later described the cancellation of the V.1000 as '...the biggest blunder of all.' The decision to stop building the Vickers V.1000 long range jet ultimately left large air transport sales largely in American hands. The delay and subsequent cancellation of the Vickers V.C.7 allowed the US Boeing to catch up and to incorporate improvements on the 707. Thus, with no trans-Atlantic competition, the market was given over to the US Boeing 707.

The brief encounter with the V.1000/V.C.7 episode provides an insight into an era when seamless knowledge for strategic continuity was the norm. The close liaison between the UK government-owned airline BOAC, the RAF and the Ministry of Aviation/Supply agencies and Rolls-Royce indicates to a very high degree the level of the UK government's knowledge and understanding of technical capability in relation to operational requirements for economic expansion and the defence of the realm. The British government of the day, through its various agencies, had full access to and was well versed in the knowledge of the UK aviation industry's technical capabilities and its aspirations. The UK government was therefore in a position to nurture and grow the strategic capability or to possibly trade away the advantage. If the advantage was traded away, then what did the government receive in the way of compensation or offset?

The transatlantic-capable Vickers V.C.7 prototype was broken up and a less capable competitor was given the ball. Nevertheless, Rolls-Royce developed the Conway by-pass engine for the Vickers VC-10, the Douglas DC-8 and the Boeing 707. The Rolls-Royce Conway engines gave the US Boeing 707 transatlantic capability. In service the Rolls-Royce Conway was to establish operational records which challenged and overhauled the US aero-engine maintenance paradigm.

Although the Conway's performance was superior to the Pratt & Whitney JT-4 and JT-3 turbojet aero-engines, the British engine did not sell among the US airlines, which appeared to have waited for an equivalent US-produced engine. P&W, as it appears was its custom, borrowed the bypass idea and produced a multi-stage fan to fix to its JT3 and this fix enabled P&W to provide the JT3D turbofan version. As the technical editor of *Flight* noted at the time:

> Spurred on by the prospect of mounting competition from Rolls-Royce with an inherently more efficient powerplant, the American company produced a front fan engine, capable of being built up from the JT3C turbojet by a kit of parts and instructions sent to operators at a major overhaul.

A significant feature of Rolls-Royce's bid to power the Boeing 707 with its advanced Conway bypass engine was that the Rolls-Royce developed bypass technologies caused Pratt & Whitney to drastically change their aero-engine to something aping the Conway. This in itself is a significant testament to the technological and performance superiority of the British engine. That the genesis of the idea for the engine underwrote UK Air Ministry specification B.35/46 is of equal significance as it indicates, with a very high degree of accuracy, the advanced technical and commercial threats the UK aviation industry, supported by the UK Sovereign government, posed to its US contemporaries. Yet despite Herculean efforts to overcome the unnatural obstacles, the UK company did not succeed. Rolls-Royce did manage to get its R.Co Conway onto 69 out of the 1,519 US Boeing 707 aircraft, but perhaps unsurprisingly Pratt & Whitney supplied the rest. Again, there was a time delay which impacted on the Conway that eventually benefited the US and enabled the US P&W corporation to incorporate improvements to its engine and eventually succeed in the market.

The licensed copying of the Rolls-Royce Nene and Tay aero-engines by Pratt & Whitney helped to establish the US company in the new jet engine and gas turbine aviation markets. The P&W company's adoption of Bristol's two spool concept along with the US company's adoption of Rolls-Royce's bypass technologies were further evidence of the US's strategic dependence on the UK's advanced aero engine technologies.

As is evident, the response to the commercial challenges posed by Rolls-Royce to US aviation interests was exhibited in the Pratt & Whitney Corporation's delay and adoption of UK aero-engine technologies. However, for the US to continue to borrow and adopt UK technologies was always going to highlight the over-reliance of the US on the UK. Such an over-reliance on the UK by the US was an obvious political weakness and an evident flaw in the US's industrial capability. With the US keen to protect its own nascent jet industry so that it might exploit the new technology and guard against economic decline, then perhaps the only way forward for the US was to impose itself politically on transatlantic transnationalism. Perhaps after the V.1000/V.C.7 debacle, the US in the future would deem that no competition would be necessary?

The match was, in this instance, lost to P&W but Rolls-Royce was by no means out of the game. With the Conway out of the commercial competition, Rolls-Royce needed to up the ante in its technological battle with its US competitors. Again, Rolls-Royce looked to its very capable designers and engineers to provide advanced technologies in the company's bid to secure commercial success and financial reward for its very capable efforts. Would the Americans wait for the introduction of the next British engine before responding with their challenge or would the Americans try to get even by setting the pace of engine development?

The RB.178

According to Cownie, Gunston, Hayward and the UK Department of Trade and Industry, the roots of the advanced RB.178 go back to 1961 when Rolls-Royce officially initiated work on a high by-pass ratio aero-engine as a replacement for the Conway.

Eltis and Wilde suggest that the RB.178 programme was begun in 1960. However, what these early dates in the RB.178's life indicate is that Rolls-Royce wasted no time in pursuing the lost Conway battle and set to work on the next technology leap.

Early details of the RB.178's projected performance first came into the public light in November 1964. Sir Denning Pearson confirmed that the RB.178 aero-engine was to have a specific fuel consumption of 10 per cent less than that of the Conway, a minimum thrust of 25,000 lb, was projected to cost in the order of £15 million to develop to the production stage and could be ready within four years from go ahead. In addition, *Interavia* revealed the Conway successor aero-engine was to develop a maximum take-off thrust of 25,000 lbst at an engine speed of 9,260 rpm, and the projected weight of the complete power-plant with nacelle was to have been 6,300 lb.

According to *Flight*, the twin-shaft 25,000 lbst RB.178 was seen as the ideal power-plant for the BEA 150–200 seat subsonic airliner project, a must for the Super VC10, and a candidate for the BAC/SUD Galeon air bus project. In the UK, as a response to BEA's requirement for an air bus, Hawker Siddeley Hatfield produced two studies for a twin RB.178-powered aircraft the first was the HS.132, with the engines located on the aft of the fuselage. The second study was the HS.134, with the two engines mounted under the wings.

The UK Competitor: The B.S.123

Pedigree of a turbofan
Part of the Hawker Siddeley Group was a 50 per cent share holding in Bristol Siddeley Engines Limited (BSEL). On 1 April 1959, Bristol Siddeley Engines Limited was formed from the merger of Bristol Aero-Engines and Armstrong Siddeley Motors. These were the aero-engine manufacturing companies of the Bristol Aircraft Company and the Hawker Siddeley Group.

The Bristol Siddeley company designed, built and maintained aero-engines at Coventry and Bristol. The heritage of BSEL included Metropolitan Vickers's work on the F.2, the UK's first axial turbojet, which in 1946 formed the basis of the F.9 Armstrong Siddeley Sapphire turbojet. BSEL's heritage also included the Armstrong Siddeley ASX, first run in 1943.

Dr A. A. Griffiths and Hayne Constant, together with A. R. Howell at the RAE from 1926 onwards, originally developed the axial compressor cascade blade technology that would be utilized in the F.9 Sapphire. When their work on compressors was combined together with Dr Smith's outstanding contributions to aerodynamics in the F.2 compressor they led to the Sapphire's axial compressor being recognised by a clear margin as the best in the world. Whyte in his paper on the 'Development of a Turbojet Engine for Aircraft Propulsion' stated: 'The Sapphire was technically well ahead of all its rivals in Great Britain and the USA …' (Whyte)

In 1946, prior to their merger with Armstrong Siddeley, Bristol Aircraft Engines had begun studies that resulted in the BE.10 Olympus, the world's first twin-shaft, two-spool turbojet. According to Tony Butler the BE.10 was proposed for the Bristol Type.172 and a diagram of the engine type has been dated at 28 May 1946, the same year as the UK Air Ministry issued specification B.35/46. I suggest that the date indicates the advanced thinking behind the BE.10 design.

The twin spool BE.10 was first run on 16 May 1950 and achieved a thrust of over 10,000 lbst against a design of 9,140 lbst. The advanced technology Bristol Olympus BE.10 engine entered service with the RAF on the Avro Vulcan in 1955 at a power rating of 11,000 lbst The Olympus quickly established new world records; in one instance, an Olympus-powered

Canberra set a world altitude record (jet) of 65,876 ft. The development of the BE.10 Olympus engine programme resulted in a number of new technologies and these spurred the development of a host of innovative Bristol bypass and ducted aero-engines. In 1956 the Olympus was redesigned to take account of Bristol's advanced compressor technologies. For the same intake diameter, the mass airflow was increased from 180lbs > 240lbs, while overall pressure ratio remained 12, providing a significant increase in thrust of 17,000 lbst. The higher thrust Olympus entered service with the Vulcan in July 1960.

The BE.10 low pressure compressor contributed to ducted fan studies on the BE.29, the BE.37, and the BE.42 and the subsequent engineering gains were fed directly into the Bristol BE.53 high by-pass aero-engine project. Gordon Lewis was responsible for compressor design and development on the BE.10 and it was his idea to combine the BE.10's LP compressor with the gas generator of the Orpheus to form what would become the BE.53 (Pegasus).

By 1958, the BE.48 had developed into the BE.53, later to be known as the Pegasus vectored thrust engine for the Hawker P.1127 (Kestrel). The BE.53 used the two-spool concept, with the first three stages of the BE.10 Olympus low pressure compressor forming the high by-pass ratio turbofan. Later models would feature additional novel technologies such as contra-rotating turbines and an overhung fan that dispensed with inlet guide vanes. The novel high bypass turbofan's features such as twin shafts, a multi-stage fan with low pressure compressor, and no IGVs are indicative of many modern-day high bypass turbofans.

In the late 1950s and early 1960s, BSEL designers and engineers used their combined talents and resources to take the BE/BS.53 vectored thrust turbofan design a stage further. BSEL developed the BS.53 engine for a number of aircraft proposals and the BS.53/16 with Plenum Chamber Burning (put simply, combustion in the front nozzles) was allotted the designation BS.100 on 28 April 1961.

Between April 1961 and April 1965, Bristol Siddeley designed and developed the BS.100 high bypass turbofan to the pre-production stage for the Hawker Siddeley P.1154 supersonic Harrier. The P.1154 was to have provided fleet air defence for the Royal Navy, the supersonic aircraft being capable of high interception speeds combined with the versatility of V/STOL recovery on the Royal Navy's new CVN.1 aircraft carriers.

The Bristol Siddeley 100 engine was also submitted to power competing aircraft designs in a 1962 NATO competition for a supersonic V/STOL fighter. For the Hawker P.1154 supersonic Harrier, the engine was designated the BS.100/9. This version of the engine had a bpr of 1.2:1 and was designed to produce 33,070 lbst. BSEL also provided the BS.100/3 engine for the Republic/Fokker D24. For this aircraft, the engine had a bpr of 1:1 and produced a thrust of 37,080lbst. Both engines operated at T4 temperatures of +1400°C.

The twin-shaft BS.100/3 development engine utilized innovative technologies which had been introduced by BSEL on the BS.53 series of high by-pass ratio turbofans. These included the advanced compressor technologies from the Sapphire and the Olympus, radical technologies such as contra-rotating low and high pressure compressor-turbines, which countered gyroscopic imbalance, and a highly advanced two-stage fan overhung ahead of the front bearing which dispensed with the need for inlet guide vanes. Together with the addition of Plenum Chamber Burning, the BS100/8 was designed to produce thrusts in excess of 33,000 lbst.

The design and development experience involved on the BS.100 programme, in particular the low pressure compressor, together with high bypass fan and high engine temperatures, would have placed Bristol Siddeley in a very advantageous position, technically, to read across the technologies for commercial use in a large high by-pass aero-engine. An advanced high temperature gas generator would be necessary to drive a large fan moving very large masses of relatively slow air for the production of high thrusts associated with high bypass ratios.

Running alongside the development of the military uses for the new high bypass aero-engine technology were considerations for its commercial use. *Flight* reported, in January 1965, that two obvious Bristol Siddeley high by-pass ratio engine projects which would read across for a commercial air bus were an un-vectored BS.100 or a fanned Olympus. However, because the addition of a front fan to the Olympus would make the engine too large, a fanned Olympus was likely to have one or two remote exhaust driven fans. This description of a fanned Olympus sounds as though Bristol Siddeley were considering the development of a three-shaft high by-pass ratio turbofan with the fans located on a separate stage from the two-shaft Olympus.

Geoff Wilde acknowledged Lionel Haworth, who had moved to BSEL from Rolls-Royce in 1963, in his lecture 'The Origins of the RB.211' as the originator of the three-shaft design. Lionel Haworth originated the concept of the three-shaft engine in the 1940s while Stanley Hooker was still working for Hives. It is fair to assume that Hooker was aware of the triple shaft concept when he moved to Bristol in 1948. Later, when Haworth joined Bristol Siddeley, it is quite possible that BSEL considered using the three-shaft concept on an advanced turbofan by-pass aero-engine, such as a fanned Olympus.

In its time, the Bristol-developed BS.100/8 was the most powerful high bypass ducted fan in the world and this underlined BSEL's advanced position in the design and development of high by-pass turbofan technologies. Relatively, BSEL were several years ahead of the US with the new technology of high by-pass ratio ducted engines. BSEL's knowledge and experience in designing and producing powerful high by-pass aero-engines can be said to have been read across so that the knowledge directly, and logically, influenced the aircraft designers, the aerodynamicists and the engineers at Hawker Siddeley in their design offices and development works in Kingston (Harrier) and Hatfield (Airbus).

The connection between the advanced technologies employed in the development of high bypass ratio aero-engines and advanced airframes and aero-foils through the same organisation, such as the Hawker Siddeley group, is plainly obvious. At Kingston and Hatfield, the engine airflow and thermodynamic data on, for example, the interference values of engines, airframes and wings was critical in the design, development and the production of world beating aviation solutions such as the Harrier (BS.53 and Pegasus) and the A.300/A.300B's aft loaded wing (BS/S.123).

For the commercial airliner market, BSEL had been developing its high bypass ducted fan technology from its origins in the BE.48 and BE.53 engines and the technology was applied and tested on the BE.50 and the BE.58. The BE.58 ducted fan engine first ran in 1959 and was the engine proposed as the powerplant for the Bristol 200, a Bristol tri-jet design that competed against the de Havilland 121. The static thrust of the BE.58 civil high by-pass aero-engines ranged from 13,250 lbst to 15,530 lbst and the figures for the sfc were 0.57 and 0.63 respectively.

The BE/BS.59 series of ducted fan engine, up to 1.6:1 bpr, were designs covering a thrust range between 3,240 lbst and 13,300 lbst. These engines were proposed for the AW.660 Argosy (BE.59/7) and the Bristol 208 VTOL (BE.59/8), among other aircraft designs.

Bristol BE.10 Olympus Mk 104. (Author)

The Bristol BE.53/5. (Author)

A Bristol Siddeley Pegasus.

A Bristol Siddeley BS.100 PCB. In 1962, this was the world's most advanced military turbofan. (Author)

The BE.64 ducted fan engine of around 14,000 lbst was proposed by Bristol for the DH.121, and a scaled down version with a thrust of 11,000 lbst was the BE.64-1. The BS.72 was proposed as an 8,000 lbst ducted fan engine for the Bristol 205 Viscount replacement and the BS.74 of 12,000 lbst with a sfc of 0.48 was another proposal for the DH.121. Next came the BS.75.

In 1960, *Flight* commented: '[The BS.75] ...was carefully optimized from the start and represents a synthesis of all the best features arrived at in the investigations of earlier ducted fans.'

A Bristol Siddeley trade journal published in 1961 describes what was once a very promising engine:

> The BS 75 is another of Bristol Siddeley's high-ratio turbofan engines suitable for a variety of civil and military aircraft. It has been specified for the British Aircraft Corporation Type 107 and the Avro Type 771 airliners. As a result of the high flow ratio of 1.75:1 the engine has a 10% better specific fuel consumption [0.508lb/lbst/hr] than an equivalent conventional turbojet of the same thrust and it has a lower noise level at take-off. Further advantages of this engine are that it develops more thrust [7550lbst] for the same weight than a straight jet and it has a high ratio of take-off thrust to cruising thrust, thus enabling the aircraft to have a take-off performance rivalling that of the turboprop. The development of these engines to the high degree of reliability expected of a civil engine is being accelerated by the use of a large number of components similar to those already proven in other Bristol Siddeley engines.

At the higher thrust ratings, the larger thrust BE.58 and BS.74 high by-pass ducted engines would have competed against the Rolls-Royce RB.141 Medway as proposals for the initial de Havilland DH.121. The lower thrust BS.75 was put forward by BSEL to power the Hunting project (BAC.107), a private venture that was to become the Rolls-Royce

Spey-powered BAC1-11, the British short to medium haul successor to the commercially successful Vickers Viscount.

What this brief insight into the ducted fan design and development activity of BSEL amounts to is that Bristol Siddeley were building up a considerable amount of design knowledge and development experience with ducted fan technologies. The knowledge and experience would enable the company to propose a large very high bypass ratio turbofan for the new wide-body and air bus concepts which were starting to appear on the drawing boards of aircraft manufacturers in Europe and the US.

The Bristol Siddeley SNECMA BS.123

In 1965, further details about the UK's requirement for a large high by-pass turbofan aero-engine were provided by the British Aircraft Corporation (BAC), in which the Bristol Aeroplane Company held a twenty percent shareholding. BAC was talking with engine firms about the feasibility of a really big new aft fan in the 30,000 lb plus thrust range, with a by-pass ratio as high as 8:1. Interestingly, the same report mentioned that a combined Rolls-Royce/Bristol Siddeley venture for a large turbofan engine could not be ruled out.

BSEL under Dr Stanley Hooker had conducted its own studies for producing a large high by-pass ratio turbofan to compete with the Pratt & Whitney and Rolls-Royce projects. In June 1965, Bristol Siddeley announced the BS-SNECMA BS.123 high by-pass ratio

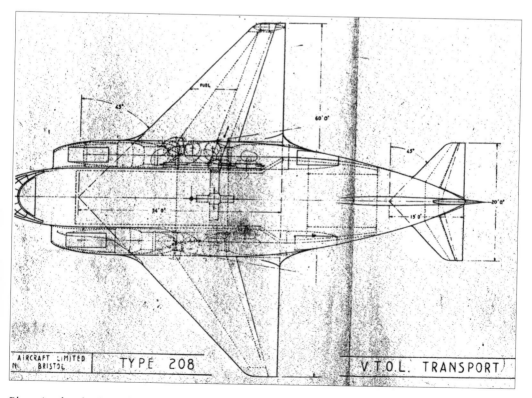

Blueprint for the Bristol Type 208 VTOL transport, which was to be powered by BE/BS.59 engines. (RRHT)

Harrier model in wind tunnel test.

Hawker Siddeley Harrier.

turbofan in the 30–40,000 lb thrust class aimed at the European air bus and the SUD/BAC Galion. The BSEL project study P.S.225 document provides a description of the engine's performance: 'The BS 123/3 is a 3:1 by-pass ratio "front fan" engine giving 30,000 lb sea level static thrust …Bristol Siddeley's background experience with Olympus and Pegasus engines was utilised to the full in its design.'

For the large fan high bypass BS.123, Bristol Siddeley teamed up with SNECMA, their partners on the Olympus 593 for Concorde and the M.45 Mars series of aero-engines. Between them they offered the airframe companies the BS.123/3 turbofan design with a by-pass ratio of 3:1 that was, by October 1965, projected to produce 35,000 lb thrust. This engine project was offered to SUD-Aviation for use on the Galion. It was to have had the Concorde hot end and a BS.100-type fan. Bristol Siddeley/SNECMA, by offering the BS.123, had raised the ante in the high by-pass stakes and declared that their aero-engine would deliver an SFC at least 15 per cent better than current values. The manufacturers' focus on the importance of fuel consumption performance is an indication of what type of aircraft they were aiming to supply the engine for.

The twin-spool BS.123/8 was a direct competitor for the same long range markets as was the Rolls-Royce RB.178 and the GE TF-39. Both the short cowl and long cowl options on the BS.123 were designed for the front mounting links and mounting trunnions located on the engine fan casing and this appears to follow the same front mounting adopted by both GE and P&W for the TF39 on the Lockheed C-5A and the JT9D for the 747.

The BS.123 studies culminated in an engine project that was predicted to cost some £450,000 per unit, but BSEL considered this to be too expensive to go it alone. In the same time frame that Bristol Siddeley/SNECMA produced the project studies for the BS.123 series of engines, over in the US the General Electric company's TF39, with a bpr of 8:1, was announced as the winner of the US DoD-sponsored engine competition to power the CX-HLS (Lockheed C5-A).

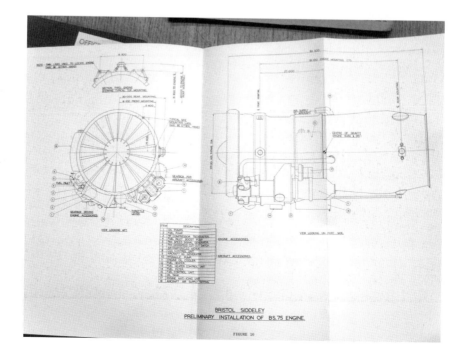

GA drawing
of Bristol
Siddeley
BS.75.
(RRHT)

The Bristol Siddeley BS.75 Turbofan at R-RHT Derby. The initial engine ran on the test bed in January 1961. (Author)

By mid-1966, Bristol Siddeley and SNECMA had dropped their BS.123 plans in favour of a joint arrangement to produce a European version of the planned P&W JT9D. When BSEL, together with the French state-owned company SNECMA, negotiated a license in 1966 to produce the Pratt & Whitney JT-9D, a significant feature of the agreement was Pratt's request that BSEL and SNECMA each take responsibility for and produce a high pressure compressor suitable for use in the JT-9D.

The Problem with Pratt's

The Pratt & Whitney JT9D was a development of the US Department of Defense-sponsored STF.200/JTF14. The P&W STF.200/JTF14, with a bypass ratio of 3.6:1 and an overall pressure ratio of 20:1, was the state of the US corporation's HBR art and as such it was the engine put forward by P&W for the USAF's CX-HLS strategic transport. It is interesting that Pratt's would later admit that they were having severe problems with the high pressure compressor on the JT9D. This problem probably affected the STF.200/JTF14 engine for the USAF and possibly indicated why the GE TF39 was chosen for the CX-HLS instead of the P&W offering.

With the USAF's rejection of the P&W engine and Pratt's subsequent decision to commercialise their HBR design, the US corporation asked BSEL and SNECMA to design and build a high pressure compressor. According to the business proposal:

The participation of the two companies [BSEL and SNECMA] in the development by Pratt & Whitney of the JT9D engine; this phase commenced on the 1st July 1966 and concerns the design of a high-pressure compressor of high performance.

From the timing, I suggest that the design of the P&W commercial JT9D for the 747 was started in April 1966 to coincide with the engine's selection by Pan American. I also suggest that to coincide with the inclusion of BS/SNECMA, the confirmed and formal launch of the P&W-powered Boeing 747 was announced in July 1966. However, it does appear odd that Boeing and Pan American had selected an engine design which by P&W's own admission was likely to be deficient in the performance of the high pressure compressor. Nevertheless, by July, with the inclusion of both SNECMA and BSEL, together with the latter's excellent performance record of high pressure compressor design, P&W decided that the first JT9D engine would be ready to begin testing in December 1966. Whereas the BSEL and SNECMA compressors were scheduled for delivery by January 1968, this suggests the P&W JT9D was tested for over a year without the beneficial performance of a BSEL-designed high pressure compressor.

What this accumulation of information suggests is that the BSEL high bypass ratio ducted fan, shaft, bearing and compressor technologies may have been at least equal to or better than their competitors'. This further extends an argument that Rolls-Royce may have bought BSEL for a number of reasons, which may have included the denial of the BSEL high by-pass technologies to Pratt & Whitney.

Such a view fits with the suggestion that Rolls-Royce was aware, as was A. A. Griffiths, of the technical performance advantages of high by-pass ratios on aero-engines, this despite a commercial argument in favour of a low ratio in the order of parity between bypass and core engine airflow. The received view is that in 1966, Rolls-Royce bought BSEL to thwart the US P&W corporation in its bid to enter the home market on the European A.300. The collaborative arrangement between BSEL, SNECMA and P&W can be seen as evidence of the politics of interdependency and duplication at work: there would be no duplicated effort and the UK would have been dependent on a US-designed high by-pass ratio aero-engine, had the European JT9D gone ahead.

It is interesting to note that in a similar time frame to the early development of the BE.53, the US Pratt & Whitney corporation used the Bristol idea of positioning a large multi-stage low pressure compressor so as to form a bypass engine and, as if by magic, out of their hat popped the JT3D and JT8D turbofan versions of their previously inefficient turbojets. Curiously, neither the Bristol Siddeley nor Rolls-Royce engines in the BS.64, BS.75, and Medway categories were produced, even though their US contemporary the Pratt & Whitney Corporation produced a similar engine, the JT8D, which sold in the thousands. Had Bristol's been courted by the US corporation and promised the Earth for their advanced compressor and bypass technologies? Were Bristol's sold the dream of thousands of Bristol-produced Pegasus engines powering military and commercial aircraft if only Bristol would help out P&W in its battle against Rolls-Royce? Looking back, it is clear that the Derby Conway fell by the commercial wayside in the face of the new, improved US P&W engine and that the Bristol Pegasus never achieved the military and commercial success its designers felt it deserved. Perhaps what is also becoming clear is that the UK aero-engineers were striving to achieve success in the dominant US market but at the expense of an engineered battle between themselves that would result in a pyrrhic victory.

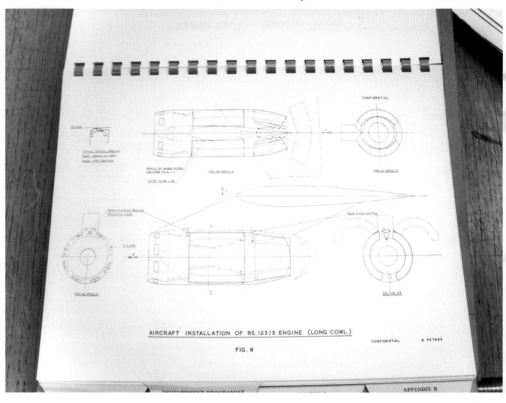

Project study diagram of BS.123/3 with long cowl. (Author via RRHT)

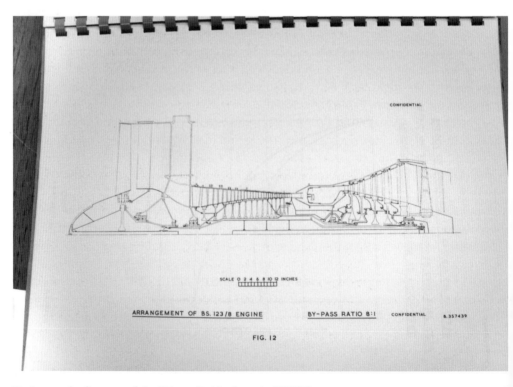

Project study diagram of the BS.123/8. (Author via RRHT)

The RB.178 Technology Demonstrator

In 1963 Adrian Lombard, aware that the Conway had lost the battle against the P&W JT3, proposed a successor engine. Subsequently, in April 1965, the main board of Rolls-Royce was asked to authorise the production of what would become the RB.178 technology demonstrator. The company went ahead with the project and under the leadership of Lombard built the twin-spool demonstrator, with the Ministry of Aviation agreeing to contribute 50 per cent of the costs up to a maximum of £450,000. Altogether, the UK government was to contribute £1.3 million towards the development of the RB.178, which suggests that the overall development cost of the state-of-the-art RB.178 was £2.6 million.

As a comparison, the GE and P&W companies were awarded nearly $20 million by the US DoD to develop and build the TF39 and the STF200 technology demonstrators. This comparison appears to indicate that the cost to the UK government of the Rolls-Royce RB.178 was good value for money. With the RB.178 appearing to be reliably inexpensive, the UK project's cost performance also posed a significant threat to the generously funded US projects. The RB.178 was built on the reliable and economic advantages inherent in the Conway and given that engine's heritage, the new engine's performance looked certain.

The Development of the RB.178

Eltis and Wilde, in their paper on the development of the RB.211, described the RB.178-14 as a two-shaft experimental demonstration engine designed to produce 27,000 lb static take off thrust. The engine in its 25,000lbst guise had a by-pass ratio of 2.3:1 and was proposed for the Vickers Superb. An assumption I make is that the RB.178's core power generation unit or boiler would have been designed and suitably scaled to drive an advanced low pressure fan across a range of three-shaft high by-pass ratio engines, such as the ATE family.

Publicly, there were a number of versions of the RB.178: the 14-, the -16, the -51 and the -61, the engines varying in thrusts and bypass ratios. One version of the RB.178 was the engine proposed for the Superb DB.265 VC-10. The RB.178 designated the -16 series appears to have been the engine specifically designed for the super-super VC-10 (DB.265), four of which would have powered the high capacity transatlantic airliner. Despite what was a very promising engine, the UK government refused it financial support and the engine for the transatlantic DB.265 was cancelled on 11 May 1966.

Although Rolls-Royce scheduled testing of the two-shaft RB.178 high bypass engine to begin in March or April 1966, the engine is said to have been run for the first time in July 1966, 53 weeks after the authority to start work was given in early 1965. Uncertainty surrounds the date of the first run of the RB.178. Whether this was in time for the Boeing spring visit of 1966 or whether it was in June 1966 is open to debate.

The RB.178 high bypass engine had been conceived as a larger and more powerful version of the Medway, which was itself a member of an optimized family of advanced two-shaft bypass engines that included the Conway and the Spey. However, and unlike the military-derived Conway, the commercially developed Medway and the RB.178 were destined to remain on the ground. There are perhaps many reasons why the RB.178 failed to take off and chief among them was the refusal of Boeing to accept the Rolls-Royce engine on the transatlantic 747.

With the UK government's cancellation of the transatlantic Vickers DB.256 Superb in May 1966, Rolls-Royce's Lombard ordered the RB.178 to be up-scaled for the diligent pursuit of the Boeing 747 engine contract. Rolls-Royce engineers and designers ardently pursued the opportunity to engine Boeing's 747 but all their hard work and effort was to be in vain. In April 1966, Boeing and Pan Am selected the US Pratt & Whitney JT9D engine for their 747 and in doing so they selected a US engine which was in many ways similar to that which was offered by Rolls-Royce.

Adrian Lombard, I suggest, with the selection of the US engine, could see the pieces of the long game falling into place and at that point he ordered the development of the ATE three shaft engine to take over from the projected RB.178 for Boeing. I suggest that at the time of the selection of the P&W engine for the Boeing 747, Lombard had already anticipated the outcome and was already running two separate engine developments, one as a foil and one as insurance against the other.

The advanced technologies employed on the engine would crossover into the three-shaft engine programmes. As such, the RB.178 engine's significance is manifold not least because the engine's appearance at the time gave an outward impression of the advanced state of Rolls-Royce's high bypass ratio engine art. Another interesting feature of the RB.178 is that like its BSEL and US contemporaries, it was to incorporate a front of pylon engine mounting on the fan case.

Although aviation historians today portray the RB.178 as a failure, the contemporary reports suggest that the engine appeared to have successfully achieved its initial design objectives. By producing 25,000 lbst and generating a 25 per cent reduction in specific fuel consumption, the engine was on target according to Sir Denning's earlier publi-

The two-shaft
RB.178 on test.
(RRHT Bristol)

nnouncement. The RB.178's operating performances would have been significant and material increases over the comparative performance of the RCo.43 Conway. It noteworthy that when Rolls-Royce first introduced the Conway, the engine provided operators with an fc of 0.67 against 0.92 from the competing P&W JT3 turbojet. The Rolls-Royce Conway also afforded transatlantic capability, a performance the US P&W JT3 was unable to reach. Bill Gunston highlighted the difference between the superior performance of the Rolls-Royce Conway and that of the Pratt & Whitney JT3. In his words: 'The contrast was startling in its magnitude.' The Conway had a significant operating performance advantage over its US competitor and the engine's superior performance caused a revolution in the commercial aviation world, forcing P&W to respond.

I suggest that the groundwork laid out and established by Rolls-Royce in the development and introduction of the revolutionary Conway had set the UK company in a favourable position relative to its US competitors. It appears that the RB.178 would have had an equally startling performance contrast over its US contemporaries, and from such a perspective the RB.178 was an engine of significant development and sales potential; perhaps the engine design was conceived as another needle? However, the RB.178 engine project could equally have been conceived by the engineers and designers at Rolls-Royce and Bristol with the complex inter-rivalry between UK aero-engineers and the equally complex transatlantic UK-US political equation in mind.

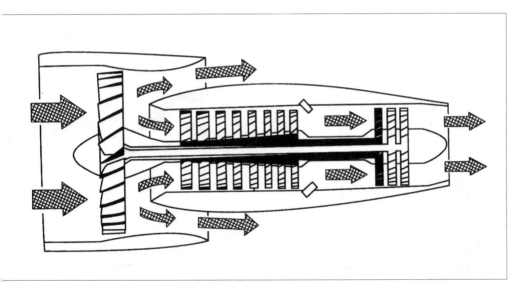

Indicative of high bypass aero-engines in use today, this diagram of the RB.178 development engine features a large fan with no inlet guide vanes and a short nacelle. (Author)

CHAPTER FOUR

THE BOEING 747

Boeing: Morphing the Orphan

The Pratt & Whitney JT9D high bypass turbofan that Boeing would use on its 747 shared many of the features of the General Electric TF39 aero-engine, which is not surprising as both companies acquired their high bypass aero-engine technologies through a US DoD funded technology development program. Both these engines' technology stemmed from the high profile US CX-HLS heavy lift aircraft program that resulted in the selection of the Lockheed C5A and GE TF39. As a result of the USAF rejection, P&W turned its attention towards the civil application of its newly acquired HBR technology. While General Electric concentrated on its high by-pass turbofan technology for the military C5A, Pratt & Whitney morphed its US DoD orphaned JT14 engine into the JT9D for the commercial 747.

Both the P&W JT9D and the GE TF39/GE1 aero-engines employed twin shaft technology and sported a large fan shrouded in a short engine cowling. In both cases the engines had their engine accessory drives mounted on the low pressure compressor casing section. The

The prototype Boeing 747 in flight. (RAeS)

heory behind using short cowlings for these new technology engines was to minimise weight and drag and therefore to optimize aircraft performance.

Boeing, in its efforts to design a fast aircraft able to cruise at 625mph, would not compromise with the 747's brochure performance. Hence it was essential that drag be kept to a minimum and one aspect of this requirement was a short, lightweight and low drag cowling for the new technology engines.

In commercial terms, as Klaus Hunecke indicates, 'Economic requirements therefore dictate that the engine intake must be a low-drag, lightweight construction, that is carefully and exactly manufactured.' Hunecke also identifies that because '[the] many requirements are conflicting, the final intake design must necessarily be a compromise. However beneficial a thin intake is for high speed cruising flight performance at take off or even low speed flight will be greatly degraded'.

Tests for both the TF39 and the JT9D started on the respective manufacturers' bench and then, as respective versions of the engines became available, the testing moved into the air on board a USAF B52. In both cases, the new high bypass turbofan engine replaced two of the Boeing B52's inboard engines. The initial test engines experienced difficulties, as all new technology acquisition programmes do. But for Boeing and Pratt & Whitney, the problems they experienced were viewed in the public eye. Likewise, GE's engine also suffered problems but these were, by and large, kept at a safe distance from the enquiring public eye because the TF39/C5A was a military programme.

In 1968, the P&W JT9D turbofan, cowled in Boeing's separately designed nacelle and pod, was to encapsulate and perhaps define the problems between the aero-engine and airframe manufacturers. The learning curve for Boeing and Pratt & Whitney was public and highly visible. GE and Lockheed on the C5A would have most likely experienced engine problems similar to those witnessed on the 747 program, as both engines originated from and shared the same technology base. As the number of hours built up in the test programme, the 747's deteriorating performance became more pronounced. Boeing's inability to get test aircraft into the air because of inoperative engines was a highly visible instance of engine failure. The engines were not performing on the wing as the manufacturer promised they would.

The received view is that Boeing only started to receive data on engine ovalization after the 747 had been flight tested for hundreds of hours. An article in *Aviation Week & Space Technology* from September 1969 indicates that the engine problems were known to Boeing long before the 747's maiden flight:

> The engine problems began to surface when Pratt & Whitney experienced deceleration stalls while flying a JT9D on a Boeing B52 (AW&ST JULY 22 1968) and they became more sharply defined as data from the flight test program began to pour in.

Boeing tried to disguise these findings by saying that the problems only revealed themselves after hundreds of flight hours of 747 testing. According to Sutter,

> P&W is experiencing an aerodynamic problem in the engine. In countering an earlier surge problem, he said, the engine company 'doctored' the match between the turbines and the compressor, opening up some turbine area to improve the flow. This was designed to achieve a modest noise improvement, 'with some loss of efficiency and weight increase' Sutter said.

Other engine problems included the appearance of fatigue cracks in the engine shaft o
early JT9D engine versions (*AW&ST*, May 1968) which grounded the test fleet and cos
precious flight time.

Brian Rowe commented of the Boeing 747's testing problems, indicating that th
problems were as much the fault of P&W as they were of Boeing but that P&W's effort
to increase engine thrust were in response to an overweight 747:

> Not only had the 747 gotten heavier than planned, Pratt & Whitney was unable to raise
> the engine thrust to the level initially required by Pan Am. At full power, the engine
> casings were distorting from a perfect circle into an oval, allowing enough leakage around
> the various engine stages to reduce thrust and increase fuel consumption. Pan American
> refused to accept delivery of the aircraft until the engines met their specifications, and, at
> one point, Boeing had more than 30 undeliverable 747s parked on the ramp with huge
> concrete blocks hanging under their wings in place of the missing engines.

Mathew Lynn wrote that Boeing had acknowledged in early 1969, that 'the main problem
was the engine. Boeing executives calculated that their stockpile of engineless, useless Jumbo
would have burnt their way through the entire net worth of the company before then'.

In the official US history of the 747, NASA notes that:

> Boeing were hanging concrete blocks on 747s coming off the production line in 1969.
> Prior to this in 1968 Boeing used 87 engines in testing the 747 and destroyed 60 of those.
> At one time Boeing could only manage to get just one 747 (out of 5) test aircraft into the
> air because there were so few working engines.

Bill Gunston, in the fourth edition of his excellent history of the jet and gas turbine
aero-engines *The Development of Jet and Turbine Aero Engines*, described the problem:
affecting the 747's aero-engines:

> Engine problems were many and serious. The first major impact was that, as power was
> applied on take off, the thrust was transmitted via the rear mount, the front fan case mount
> being floating: the engine bent nose down, the casings distorted from circular to oval and
> wide gaps appeared in one plane, blade rubs occurred at right angles.

Boeing, according to Steiner, without a doubt had a serious and very stubborn problem. The
root of the 747's engine and nacelle problems were in the design of the engine mounting
chosen by Boeing. For the new high by-pass aero-engine, Boeing decided that only one
thrust mount would be required and that it was to be located on the fan nacelle. This might
have seemed to be a suitable solution for dealing with the enormous loads exerted toward
the aircraft from the engine, which derived most of its thrust from the fan. However, in
operation the Boeing nacelle pivoted about its mounting axis, which was located off o
the engine's centre of gravity, causing case deflection or ovalisation. Another problem wa:
located within the engine. Shaft coupling on the JT-9D in addition distorted the engine
casings, causing gaps and significant loss of engine performance.

By the middle of 1969, with the Pan Am delivery date looming large and with no prospec
of a solution for the aluminium behemoth's deficient performance, both Boeing and Pratt &

hitney were squaring up to one another. In an effort to apportion blame, each corporation
dged $100 million dollar lawsuits and sued the other for the aircraft's lack of brochure
erformance, which was a result of cowling ovalization, shaft coupling, mounting difficulties,
board exhaust gas ingestion and crosswind induced compressor surging.

During the highly publicised spat between Boeing and P&W, their engineers had been
esperately trying to find a solution to the publicly known ovalization problems since the
iddle of 1969. Later in the same year, engine noise was also a major problem as the FAA
fused to certificate for airline use the 747s powered by the early JT9D.

By the time the delivery date arrived when Boeing was contracted to supply Pan
merican with the 747, Pan Am refused to take delivery of the aircraft until its performance
eficiencies had been resolved. Pan Am had to promise its shareholders that the operation
f the 747 would not negatively impact on the airline's financial performance.

A solution for the Pratt &Whitney JT9D was eventually found that allowed a reduction
the engine's power loss but not before Boeing was if not financially bankrupt then
chnically at the end of its tether.

Lynn (1989) argues that Boeing went beyond its financial limits:

Later during the development of the 747 Boeing literally ran out of money while developing
the airplane. The net worth of Boeing in 1969, the book value by which the bankers could
measure the security of their loans should the worst happen and the plug have to be pulled,
was $796 million. It already owed well over that, and the bankers were worried that they
might never be repaid.

reflection of the immense scale of the problems P&W were causing Boeing are the pictures from
te 1969 and early 1970 depicting Boeing's Washington airfield stacked up with cement laded and
operative 747s. The picture above from early 1970 shows the engineless hulks which were worthless
the airlines and financial millstones around the neck of Boeing. (PRM)

As John Newhouse has pointed out in *The Sporty Game*, it is not unheard of in the aviation industry that a company bets its entire worth on a program. Usually the company has taken a considered gamble that the technology it is seeking to acquire is not beyond its reach and that the markets are ready and willing to utilise the new technology to cater for their growing needs and ambitions, to outwit their competition and to pay healthy prices for the privilege to do so. The risks are beyond those normally acceptable to commercial financers; perhaps better returns might be had from playing roulette in Monte Carlo.

However, both Boeing and P&W positioned themselves politically, financially and technically in an over-reach situation. Their strategy in commercial terms seemed to be paying off as Pan American's competitors ordered the 747 to keep up with them. Boeing even took an increased deposit of 50 per cent from its customer airlines at about $1 million per aircraft, and with 140 aircraft on order, Boeing was sitting on a cash mountain of nearly $1.5 billion (1970 prices).

Technically Boeing was compromised, not least because the path chosen by its staff for the engine nacelle, pod and mounting designs were seriously flawed. Politically, Boeing and P&W had positioned themselves asymmetrically in relation to the White House politics of Johnson and McNamara and therefore could not rely on help from that quarter, while financially Boeing had used up all its credit on Wall Street. Just how did Boeing survive?

The Boeing company perhaps received a reprieve, possibly granted at the highest level of authority, perhaps the same authority which had granted its bemused approval to Allen and Trippe in the first instance? If such a scenario did occur then perhaps it might be argued that it set the precedent for Lockheed's Congressional support for financial assistance in 1971.

Boeing failed to make any 747 deliveries to Pan Am to enable the airline to begin service in 1969. It had forecast to deliver 747s that would generate $80 million revenues (at $1 million deposit and purchase price of say an average of $20 million, then Boeing could have been expecting to deliver eight of the 747 aircraft in December 1969).

By mid-1970 the number of engineless, useless 747s that were stood on the grey apron had risen to over thirty. The much publicized unacceptable noise levels and deficient operating performance problems of the JT-9D turbofan held up 747 certification and airline acceptance. In an effort to allay the fears of the airlines who had ordered the 747, Boeing said that they would fix the problem; however, the 747s for Pan Am and TWA would be initially below service specification.

Boeing did eventually find a solution to most of the ovalization problems caused by the shorter engine cowling with the addition of a 'Y' bracket or strut that was fitted retrospectively.

The L1011 and DC-10 utilize ¾-length pods for their wing mounted HBR engines which are visibly different from the shorter pods used on early 747s. Later versions of the 747 use a ¾-length pod, and the adoption by Boeing of a revised pod suggests that the ¾-length pod had solutions, within its design, that addressed the ovalization problems experienced by the early Boeing 747s and their related shortfall in operating performance.

CHAPTER FIVE

A. A. LOMBARD:
TAKING ON US CURTIS-WRIGHT PROTECTIONISM

Adrian Lombard, until his untimely death at the early age of 52 on 13 July 1967, was Rolls-Royce's Director of Engineering. He was not university trained but he did display a natural and phenomenally brilliant instinct for engineering supreme solutions, a natural instinct that advanced and guided the development of the jet and gas turbine engine.

Originally, Adrian Lombard came to Rolls-Royce from Rover Barnoldswick, where he was working on the Whittle W2/B. After the transfer of Rover's work on the Whittle jet engine to Rolls-Royce was completed, Lombard worked alongside Sir Stanley Hooker in the development of the Welland gas turbine. After Hooker's sad departure from Rolls-Royce to Bristol Aircraft in late 1948, Lombard's technical brilliance shone 'as one of the world's greatest gas-turbine engineers and [he] was eventually to become a main board director and Director of Engineering of the Aero Engine Division'. (Gunston 1989)

During the negotiations for engines on the Boeing 707 programme, Lombard, a main board director of Rolls-Royce Limited, went over Sutter's head and engaged Boeing's chairman William Allen in a bid to secure the outlet for Rolls-Royce's revolutionary Conway bypass aero-engine. Because Lombard very capably traversed with ease between both the shop floor and the boardroom spheres, and had the authority to do so, this was possibly a key to Rolls-Royce gaining the Boeing 707 pod details from the Boeing executive. As is suggested by a number of historians, William Allen knew of the politics behind BOAC's choice of Rolls-Royce aero-engines and Lombard knew full well when to apply that pressure.

Historians of the received view suggest that Lombard and Sutter seemed destined not to get along. In a way, it seemed that Sutter's arrogance matched the size of the USAF's Dash-80/707 programme and it showed in the conceited way he dismissed the importance of Lombard and Rolls-Royce's new engine technology. Despite Sutter's apparent put downs and dismissal of anything British, the Americans almost immediately adopted the ducted fan by-pass concept of the Conway and employed it to create the up-rated 707 where the revised aeroplane sold in very large numbers.

So much for the dismissal of Rolls-Royce's technology by Boeing. Lombard must have been furious and so must the board of Rolls-Royce have been deeply dismayed at the apparent betrayal by Boeing and P&W. Perhaps this was the turning point for Rolls-Royce in their history of gas turbine engines as they subsequently devised a strategy to by-pass the airframe company, in this case Boeing, and its decision making process so that with future projects they would deal directly with the airlines. Rolls-Royce would challenge the US's protectionist mechanism, the Curtis-Wright patent agreement, which subjugated the power-plant manufacturer to the designs of the airframe manufacturer.

It was perhaps with his US experiences in mind that he decided as Rolls-Royce's Director of Engineering that the next aero-engine would include all the lessons of the company's US travails and incorporate all their latest advanced technologies so that Rolls-Royce would leave the US engine makers staring into the technological abyss.

Bonded to Fate

On 30 December 1965, *Flight International* published an article based on a paper given by Adrian Lombard entitled 'Jet Engine Trends'. Lombard articulated the spin off benefits for future Rolls-Royce commercial engines that employing the very latest developments in lift propulsion technology would bring.

Among the benefits identified by Lombard was the significant reduction in the length of the combustion chamber; this in turn reduced the number of bearings, which in turn reduced weight and therefore the engine cost per pound of thrust. There was also the reduction in waste weight by eliminating the bolts and flanges and replacing these with electron or laser beam welding. Such advanced manufacturing methods could reduce engine weight in a high by-pass engine by something in the region of 15 per cent.

New resin-bonded composite materials for compressor blades were expected to reduce engine weight and cost and to improve reliability.

> Composite materials under development are very suitable for cooler components, e.g., by-pass duct, the complete low pressure compressor, the front bearing housing assembly, the intermediate casing, the high pressure compressor casing and about half the high pressure rotor and stator blades.

Increased turbine entry temperatures would in turn increase the thrust per pound of air, and Lombard predicted that these would rise to about 1600°K. Increases in the cooling of blades would allow for a reduction in the size and the weight of the compressor; the smaller high pressure section would result in a higher value of by-pass ratio, which would produce a lower specific fuel consumption.

Significantly, Lombard predicted the crossover of lift jet technology to the by-pass engine, where the engine carcases would be integral with the pod structure, thus reducing engine weight. Lombard indicated that the same principle could be applied to a pair of propulsion engines mounted on an under-wing pylon. The by-pass duct would be an integral part of the permanent pod structure into which the engines are assembled.

In 1966, Adrian Lombard presented the first Royal Society Technology Lecture Aircraft: 'Power plants-past, present and future'. In his presentation, Lombard indicated that the chosen subject was a 'very topical one both because of the very advanced technology required for the design and manufacture of aero engines and of the interest which has recently centred on the aircraft industry in this country and the controversy on its future'.

Among the controversial issues highlighted by Lombard and centring on the aircraft industry was the Duncan Sandys 1957 Defence White paper. The industry had a number

Above left: An RB108.

Above right: The resin bonded composite fan blades, stators and casing on a sectioned vertical lift engine RB.162.

The sectioned vertical lift jet RB.162 and, in the background, the RB.162-4. The -4 version weighed 278 lb dry and produced 4,718 lbst, giving an unprecedented thrust to weight ratio of 17.

of setbacks, perhaps the most drastic of which was the 1957 Defence White Paper which erroneously forecast that there would be no new manned combat aircraft.

Following on from the erroneous 1957 White Paper and hard on its heels was the Labour government-inspired Plowden enquiry that Lombard criticised for causing long term uncertainty for the UK aviation industry: 'The enquiry into the aircraft industry by the Plowden Committee created a background of uncertainty that had its effect upon long term policy.'

Yet despite the apparent political efforts to stall the British aviation industry, Lombard emphasised that '...the British aero engine industry has retained its technical competitive capability...' and he demonstrated the value of competitive technologies which led the export of aero-engines and returned a major financial contribution to the UK economy: 'The value of engine exports over the last 12 years or so was nearly £M 650 excluding the engines installed in export aircraft.'

Lombard's chosen method for delivering his lecture on the complex subject of aero-engineering to his audience was to 'present a broad survey, with some emphasis on particular points...'

Lombard touched on a number of key areas in which Rolls-Royce technologies would be incorporated in its high bypass aero-engine design, illustrated in his reference to the RB.178. Among the scientific and development technologies he drew the audiences' attention to were the advances in compressor efficiency.

The Axial flow compressor was greatly improved with theory developed by Dr. A.A. Griffiths based on isolated aerofoil practice

in 1926 when he first proposed the gas turbine engine as an aircraft powerplant. This method of design, which in effect assumed two dimensional flow through each row of blades, was adopted for all axial flow work carried out during the 1940s and early 1950s.

However, Lombard indicated that with the advent of the digital computer Rolls-Royce's understanding of compressor knowledge, which had been limited to quasi three-dimensions, would allow the designers to address previous assumptions and improve performance.

Initially many simplifying assumptions were made about the airflow path - for example all radial components of velocity were neglected – but as better understanding of these phenomena became known, through the accumulation of experimental evidence more detailed procedures were adopted.

The Rolls-Royce company was investing heavily in the use and development of the large digital computer technologies to aid its own research and for its use in the aviation industry.

Lately it has become possible to provide a more complete solution to the equations of motion taking into account radial components of flow due to the curvature of the flow and the inclination of the annulus walls to the axis of the compressor and allowing for a radial variation of loss along the blade span. These methods are also being developed to include the design of the blades themselves based on the latest theories and experimental data relating to the flow in the passages between the blades.

Equally important scientific and technological advances were highlighted by Lombard in his lecture. He drew attention to turbine efficiencies which could reach 94 per cent, of the

Rolls-Royce company's commanding position in turbine cooling which allowed for higher thermal efficiency and increased combustion temperatures, of the efficient shortening of the combustor in the company's lift engine technology, the importance of design and structural efficiency and significantly of the importance of engine installation and noise.

In 1966, Lombard and Rolls-Royce once again attempted to work with the Boeing Company on the 747 project. Rolls-Royce tried to link up with General Electric in a joint production venture for the RB.178. However, and perhaps inevitably, GE refused and Sutter dismissed Rolls-Royce's revolutionary technologies which would be applied in the RB.178 as 'oatmeal'. Sutter, it appears, at almost every step took pleasure in deriding the British Rolls-Royce company's attempts to promote their advanced engine technologies for use on the US company's aircraft.

In the received view, it was Joseph Sutter, Boeing's chief engineer for the 747 programme, who supposedly prevented the British Rolls-Royce company from gaining a perch for its engines on the 747. Sutter had a history of fallouts with Lombard and Sutter's influence on those episodes is perhaps a reliable measure of the arrogance of the Boeing company and its executive, who did not negotiate with European airlines – they dealt with governments. One of the author's sources who knew Lombard said of him, 'He was a very capable engineer doing a very difficult job...'

As we will find out, the Boeing-designed nacelle and mounting for the JT9D on the 747 was to suffer many problems and cause the aircraft to fall short of its brochure stated performance. On 1 September 1969, in the US publication *Aviation Week and Space Technology*, Joseph F. Sutter acknowledged that the 747's engine performance was not expected to meet commitments as to SFC, this is 'the biggest situation we have to fight', he said.

Hyfil development blades.

CHAPTER SIX

CHANGE OF PLAN OR A CHANGE OF TACK?

In May 1966, following the selection of the P&W JT9D to power the Boeing 747, *Flight* published specifications and a detailed cutaway of the Rolls-Royce three-shaft RB.178 aero-engine.

As a response to the rejection of the RB.178, and shortly after Rolls-Royce lost out to P&W on the 747 contract, the UK Treasury-funded RB.178 technology acquisition engine was cancelled. One of the reasons given why the RB.178 was cancelled after a very short test life was that it had cost more than its budget, and therefore the UK Treasury refused to provide any more funding. Eltis and Wilde suggest three reasons why the RB.178 was short lived: 'Partly in view of the decision not to proceed with the VC10 derivative, partly for lack of research funds and partly because it was realised that the by-pass ratio was too low for other aircraft installations.' Perhaps another reason could have been a political or economic expedient to optimise the Rolls-Royce engine as a scaled response to the rigid demands of the government controlled British airlines.

Interestingly, in June 1966, *Flight* published an article titled 'The Engine Sets the Pace'. This called on Rolls-Royce to invest in a not so big RB.178 and in effect to leave the big engine market to the projected 41,000 lbst P&W JT9D. Rolls-Royce did draw up plans for scaled down versions of the RB.178 three-shaft engine; these were designated the RB.205 for the 20,000 lb thrust project and the RB.204 for the 26,000 lb thrust proposal. Perhaps echoing a similar instance, the RB.141 Medway developed for the de Havilland 121 was downsized or optimised into the Spey for the BEA downsized Hawker Siddeley Trident, which effectively left the market to the P&W JT8D powered Boeing 727.

Reflections on Strategy

Reflecting on its rejection, Rolls-Royce, in July 1966, announced through *Flight* that after the competition to supply engines for the Boeing 747, the British company had decided that it did not want to continue with the present sized RB.178 in headlong competition with the P&W JT9D engine and had chosen instead to promote a family of advanced technology turbofan engines.

Having lost the opportunity to power the Boeing 747 and facing the prospect of optimizing its engine, a further blow was dealt to Rolls-Royce when Bristol Siddeley announced a licensing deal with its US rival Pratt & Whitney to supply the JT9D.

Earlier, it had been suggested in *Flight* that Rolls-Royce and Bristol Siddeley might collaborate on the design and development of a High By-pass Ratio aero-engine. This suggests that the two companies had discussed the matter in a transatlantic context. Yet on 29 June 1966, Bristol Siddeley and SNECMA signed an agreement with Pratt & Whitney to share the building of a European JT9D as the power-plant for the proposed European air bus. Sir Denning's reply appeared anxious:

> Nevertheless, Rolls-Royce believe, to quote Sir Denning, that the 'airlines would be anxious to ensure that not all the next generation of subsonic jets are supplied by Pratt & Whitney. We have evidence that airlines would like to see Rolls-Royce as the main competitor to Pratt & Whitney.

Citing new prospects for a revised RB.178 in the US, and perhaps hinting at a Faustian pact between Labour and the US administration, Sir Denning Pearson emphasised: '...that until this question is resolved, Europe should hold its hand before selling its soul to an American engine built under licence.'

Interestingly, Sir Denning Pearson made reference to American companies working on jumbo air bus projects and arguably his reference is to Kolk and American Airlines' requirements for a Jumbo twin. Such a reference is an indication that Rolls-Royce were attuned to Kolk's requirements for an American Airlines specification and aligned with the McDonnell-Douglas wide-body design, perhaps from the very outset.

BS Duplication and Interdependency

Prior to the Rolls-Royce takeover of BSEL in 1966, Bristol Siddeley was developing its own large fan and high-bypass ducted turbofan engines. The largest, if it had gone into production, was the BS.123. This engine was cancelled by BS at about the same time that BS and SNECMA signed up to co-design and build under-licence the P&W JT9 for the European A300.

A key feature of the co-operation between BS/SNECMA and P&W was the European companies' advanced compressor technology and that the Europeans' compressor technology would 'make a major contribution to the engine for both the 747 and, without basic changes, the jumbo twin-engined airbus'.

> In discussing the BS.123 and other big fans, Pratt & Whitney admitted it was in very deep trouble with the development of the JT14, the immediate predecessor of the JT9D fan engine, destined to be used on the Boeing 747. The high pressure compressor was not performing well and the engine kept on surging.

Some Dynamics of the Rolls-Royce Merger with Bristol Siddeley

In June 1966, while Bristol Siddeley (BS) was in merger talks with Rolls-Royce, the Bristol Siddeley company and SNECMA signed heads of agreement with Pratt & Whitney with an option to take up JT9D licenses for the sale and manufacture of the engine in Europe.

Flight reported on 7 July 1966 that reactions to the proposed merger between Rolls-Royce and Bristol Siddeley (BS) were unfavourable. Rodwell Banks was strongly against the takeover of Bristol Siddeley Engines by Rolls-Royce. Yet, and despite the Plowden report's lack of support for a merger between BSEL and R-R, Hayward suggests that the merger was '…an amalgamation consistent with the Plowden report and undertaken with government encouragement'.

Whether the Labour government's support for an amalgamation between Rolls-Royce and Bristol Siddeley was tacit or overt, the result was a reduction in product duplication, a significant increase in risk due to the merged company's over reliance on its largest customer, the UK government.

The Merger

On 9 September 1966, the formal offer was sent to shareholders of the Bristol Aeroplane Company Limited; and by that date the terms had been agreed with Hawker Siddeley Group Limited in respect of its fifty per cent interest in Bristol Siddeley. The Labour government did not object to the acquisition and it was duly implemented.

By October 1966, the Rolls-Royce and Bristol Siddeley merger was complete and even though the two companies maintained separate and competing design and production centres, they were in a position to draw on each other's strengths in skills and resources.

Re-reading the Prencipe and Lazonik article, I am struck by the authors' apparent serious under-appreciation of the circumstances surrounding the BSEL takeover by Rolls-Royce Limited. The BSEL company was suffering financially and significantly so from a reduction in business because of government action due to alleged overcharging on engines and services to the UK government, charges made by the Labour government. Yet despite these significant downsides, RR still bought the company knowing that it would have to honour BSEL's outstanding commitments and support a business that had been punished and deliberately weakened by the Labour government's actions, through a reduction in business, and as a result of the reclamation of the overpaid monies.

Similarly Bowden, in my view, has underestimated or appears not to have fully engaged with the wider context surrounding the Rolls-Royce takeover/merger with Bristol Siddeley.

Another point – it has been suggested that BSEL were in a position to takeover Rolls-Royce but Pugh claims this was unlikely. Pugh provides BSEL records to support his view. However, Bristol Siddeley Engines Limited was 50 per cent owned by Europe's largest industrial company and one of the largest engineering companies in the world. The Hawker Siddeley group was presided over by T. O. M. Sopwith, and its aerospace activities accounted for a fraction of their overall business. Hawker Siddeley were much larger than Rolls-Royce, with considerably more financial muscle, and could quite easily have made a credible approach for Rolls-Royce, had they so desired. In respect to the then government's policies provoking industry consolidation, perhaps Hawker Siddeley were persuaded from extending its reach into aero-engines and in return promised the UK's part on a proposed European air bus?

In a question to Air Commodore F. R. Banks posed by *Interavia* on whether the absorption of BSEL by Rolls-Royce was the right solution, Banks replied:

The wisdom of the absorption of Bristol by Rolls could be questioned for the reason of oversize and elimination of competition in house; but I feel it was not entirely the fault of Rolls since they were considered the aero-engine bastion on this side of the Atlantic ... The enormous size of Rolls-Royce however, with nothing like the US domestic market to cater for in Western Europe, does raise the query as to whether a sufficiency of orders will emerge and where they will come from.

Banks' response suggests that the political reasoning for allowing the merger was flawed as there would not be a large enough market outside of the United States to support the enlarged Rolls-Royce company. However, Rolls-Royce were encouraged by Labour politicians to gain a necessary mass to be able to compete economically with similarly positioned US competitors, who controlled through supply 75 per cent of the Western world's commercial aviation business. Perhaps the question to be asked is what convinced the Board of Rolls-Royce to agree to the merger: Politics? Economics? Technology acquisition?

Notwithstanding the merger between Rolls-Royce and Bristol, the P&W deal between BS and SNECMA for an advanced compressor on the JT9D was allowed to continue.

CHAPTER SEVEN

ADVANCED TECHNOLOGY ENGINE FAMILY

In September 1966, at SBAC Farnborough, Rolls-Royce revealed to the world its decision to launch an advanced technology engine (ATE) family covering engine thrusts from 10,000 lbst through to 60,000 lbst. In what appears to have been a masterpiece of strategic engagement with its high by-pass aero-engine adversaries, Rolls-Royce leapfrogged them and announced the details of a series of revolutionary three-shaft ATE engine designs.

The background to the design and development of the Advanced Technology Engine family began when the first three-shaft project design study was completed by Rolls-Royce in July 1961. In 1963, the board of Rolls-Royce gave the go-ahead for the development of the advanced technology acquisition programmes. These included hyfil and titanium fan development, resin-based low pressure compressor, stators and casings, intermediate pressure compressors, advanced air cooled turbines, annular high pressure combustor, and squeeze film bearings. The scaled and full-size component test programmes together with the full-size two-shaft RB.178 engine technology demonstrator were the most visible evidence of Rolls-Royce's advanced project activities, which began rig testing in 1965.

The RB.178 demonstrator engine 'afforded valuable experience in the design and performance of the gas generator and other components', for instance on the development of the high pressure annular combustion chamber, which directly supported the development of the proposed larger ATE RB.207 variant in the 45,000 lb – 52,000 lb thrust category, an engine that was designed for the European twin engine airbus.

In support of the Rolls-Royce bid for powering the Airbus, Rolls-Royce provided a summary of its background experience in a technical brochure. This included over 68 million engine hours in commercial operation with its five basic gas turbine engines; more experience of short haul operation than any other commercial gas turbine supplier in the world; and world-wide success in aircraft engine installation. These credentials suggest that with over fifteen years of gas turbine design and operational knowledge in the harsh short haul environment, Rolls-Royce was very well placed to design a high cycle high bypass ratio turbofan for the European theatre.

Such a view is at odds with the received view as portrayed by most general aviation writers, who insist that Rolls-Royce was only focused on gaining business in the US. However, it is clear that Rolls-Royce was very keen to work with the European countries to supply an engine for the Airbus. Emphasising Rolls-Royce's European credentials and echoing the former French Air Force engineering General Zeigler's political position of resisting the colonization from the skies, Adrian Lombard clearly stated that Rolls-Royce's technical confidence and engineering experience would be shared with its European partners:

> We have offered to share the design, engineering and manufacturing programme with each of the European countries interested in supporting the European airbus. We have the talent and successful background of jet engine achievement in Europe not to require to depend on an American-licensed engine.

The Origins of the ATE

Lombard exuded confidence in Rolls-Royce's ability to better the Americans in high by-pass aero-engine technology. His confidence was built on proprietary knowledge that was intimated at in a *Flight* article entitled 'Short-Haul Engine Economics' that reviewed a paper written and presented by Eltis and Morley to the Society of Automotive Engineers in Los Angeles on 8 October 1964. In their paper they identified:

> In the future the major contributions to fuel consumption is likely to come from further increases in by-pass ratio... advances in compressor technology... improvement in pod design ... higher turbine inlet temperatures ... advances in technology of fan and turbine noise reduction ...

TRENT BACKGROUND

TURBO - PROP EXPERIENCE
High operating temperatures
39 million hours Dart – solid turbine blades
$3\frac{3}{4}$ million hours Tyne – air cooled turbine blades

SHORT HAUL EXPERIENCE
Frequent take – offs
$28\frac{1}{2}$ million hours on stage lengths below $1\frac{1}{2}$ hours

BY PASS (TURBO - FAN) EXPERIENCE
Over 6 million hours with Conway and Spey
engines in airline operation since 1960

JANUARY 1

Solid operational evidence backed up Rolls-Royce's claims for the proposed performance of the ATE RB.203 Trent. (Rolls-Royce)

In December 1964, *Flight* published highlights of Lombard's paper 'Engineering Considerations for Transport Aircraft' that he delivered to the South African RAeS in October. In his address Lombard stated the then most recent views of Rolls-Royce about the future transport aircraft engine design and development for jet feeder-liners and for short-haul mainliners. Lombard outlined many of the technologies that would feature on the future family of ATE high by-pass turbofans: '[The new] engines would have only just over half as many components as the Spey...' Lombard emphasised that there would be no need for compressor inlet guide vanes, the engine would have moderate pressure ratios, no central bearing, the by-pass duct would be made of glass-fibre and 'all accessories would be driven from one point – the high pressure rotor system'.

Cannily, one might argue that Rolls-Royce, in its battle with the US aero-engine makers, had masterfully scaled new technological heights, providing only a glimpse of the proposed scale of the changes to come. At the 1966 SBAC Farnborough show Rolls-Royce unveiled to the world its revolutionary Advanced Technology Engine (ATE) family, the junior member of which was the RB.203 Trent high by-pass ratio ducted turbofan.

The Rolls-Royce Advanced Technology Engine RB.203 Trent

The ATE Trent RB.203 high bypass ratio aero-engine design reflected the technologies which Dawson, Eltis, Huddie, Lombard, Morley, Pearson and Wilde et al had confidently predicted would be incorporated in the advanced technology engine. The ATE embraced the new scaleable technologies such as the triple-shaft architecture, a high pressure annular combustor, the extensive use of composites throughout the low pressure fan, compressor and low pressure engine casing, air cooled turbine blading, squeeze film bearings and a structurally integrated duct, with the gearbox driven from the high pressure spool and located in the nacelle.

Scientifically, the nacelle inlet and duct were calculated to provide the least aero-dynamic interference and maximum airflow to offset the penalties associated with an integrated power-plant structure.

The Trent concept. Design objectives for 3rd Generation transport engine:

1. Lighter more compact powerplant
2. Improved fuel consumption
3. Reduced number of parts, resulting in cheaper manufacturing costs and ease of overhaul
4. Use of established turbine entry temperatures
5. Conservative stressing for high cyclic life of components
6. Use of an existing gas producer
7. Adequate growth potential

The engine was aimed primarily at the short haul market as a Spey-type replacement but the technologies it utilized were particularly suitable for engines combining the high pressure ratios and the high by-pass ratios necessary for the new wide-body transport aircraft.

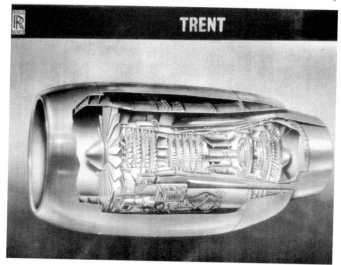

Rolls-Royce ATE Trent. TS.252.
916B. The Trent was presented
at Farnborough in September
1966. (Rolls-Royce)

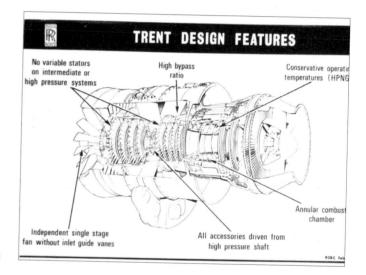

ATE RB.203 Trent design
features included the
aerodynamic gear. (Rolls-Royce)

Rolls-Royce ATE RB.203.
Author)

Specific fuel consumption was projected to be better than the then-current engines; noise reduction was also a design feature and the Trent was expected to better FAA noise proposals by a considerable margin. Advanced components, which had between 15 years and 10 million service hours, promised long life, reduced weight, reduced vibration, and a reduction in manufacturing costs. The Trent was designed for rapid turn-round and operators could expect to achieve twenty take offs per day where the engine would work a third of its life in the climb phase.

Rolls-Royce had successfully designed and developed the three shaft concept and the key ATE technologies and these were proven in the established running of the RB.203 high bypass aero-engine that began on 18 December 1967. What this suggests is that Rolls-Royce was on course for the design and development of the ATE RB.207, and that Rolls-Royce was confident the engine for the European Airbus would achieve its performance as specified and within time.

The confidence in their knowledge of gas turbines, and in their design and technical ability as exhibited by Rolls-Royce in 1966, was to be borne out in the ATE development programmes. It is because of the company's design and development engineers' confidence in their knowledge of gas turbines that I suggest that Rolls-Royce's strategy was to reveal its technologies at the very last moment. In doing so, Rolls-Royce had forced GE and P&W to commit to second generation high by-pass technologies, while Rolls-Royce leap-frogged them with its third generation of high bypass ratio advanced technology engines.

Rolls-Royce, with their advanced third generation high by-pass family of engines, would have been in a position of strength to cherry pick its business among the emerging second generation of wide body designs. Reflecting Sir Denning Pearson's position, Rolls-Royce had stayed its hand in its bid for the 747, a bid that one might argue had from the outset already been granted to P&W.

The RB.203 and RB.207: Scaling New Technological Heights

Reflecting the scale of the revolutionary changes, Rolls-Royce dropped the RB.178 engine design that directly competed with the P&W JT9D and instead pursued a family of more advanced engines based on the three-shaft ATE concept. Rolls-Royce was now concentrating on developing its three-shaft technologies for engine cycles which were better suited to high cycle airline needs as required in the European markets. The projected 60,000 lbst RB.207 that was suitable for European air bus designs was also a good match for Kolk's proposed big twin high cycle machine.

In their bid to power the 747, the US engine company Pratt & Whitney optimized the JT9D's power cycle for long range flight such as the transatlantic sector. This called for the engine's performance to reflect low cycle usage and high speed, with the majority of power time at altitude. However, the RB.207 design was optimized for high cycle short to medium haul sectors that would see the engine spending more time in climbing and descending at relatively low speeds, but requiring greater thrusts more frequently.

By November 1966, the triple-spool RB.207-01, the largest of the new scalable advanced technology turbofans from Rolls-Royce, was being offered for the Hawker Siddeley/Bregeut/Nord HBN.100 as an alternative to the JT9D and the RB.178.

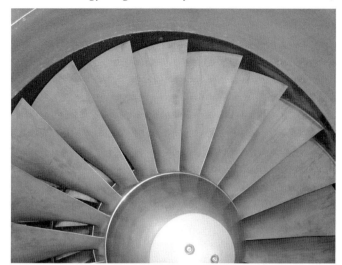

The advanced wide chord fan of the RB.203 in front of the resin composite i-p compressor blades and stators. (Author)

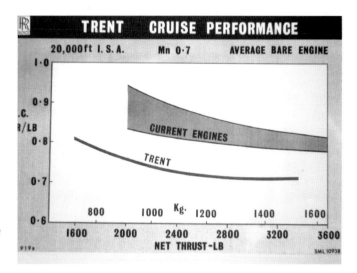

A graph showing Trent performance from a Rolls-Royce brochure, October 1966. (Rolls-Royce)

Reflecting the ATE family three shaft architecture, the RB.203 development preceded the RB.207 and the RB.211. (Rolls-Royce)

Between November 1966 and June 1967, the Rolls-Royce RB.207 formed the basis of twin engine large capacity aircraft design studies for short/medium haul in Europe and the US. In July 1967, despite Rolls-Royce's plan for a family of ATE engines, the Labour government accepted in principle the 'Dual Programme'. For a short while the Rolls-Royce board actively promoted both the RB.207 and the RB.211 engines in the US. Neither of the Rolls-Royce engines competed directly against either of its US engine competitors.

The US airframe manufacturers Lockheed and McDonnell-Douglas pursued their respective studies for a large capacity, twin turbofan-powered short to medium range airliner. Their studies followed Kolk's specification and were similar to the European conceived designs for an Airbus. Lockheed even went as far as trying to engage the Europeans in a transatlantic project to jointly produce an air bus.

Rolls-Royce ATE RB.203 Trent rear profile. Visible are the broad turbine casing, the externally mounted gearbox and accessories, and the composite i-p OGV casing. (Author)

CHAPTER EIGHT

THREE INTO TWO

Notwithstanding the commercial advantages of a 'Jumbo Twin', Kolk had, curiously and according to *Flight*, by April 1967, relaxed his dogmatic insistence on a twin-engine airbus and, as a consequence, Kolk had fallen into line with the majority of the US airlines, who saw greater advantages in a three-engine US wide-body. With the disappearance of an American project for a large twin air bus, and as a consequence the disappearance of a significant US market for the type, the Rolls-Royce RB.207 was damned.

In a similar time frame, the UK Ministry for Technology (Mintech) was attempting to build bridges between the US and UK aviation industries. As the would-be financier of an engine for a US air bus, Mintech also considered that a three-engine aircraft would be more advantageous, and was supported in its efforts by BALPA and the British Board of Trade in its attempts to change the twin-engine Airbus. Benn attempted to convince his French and German partners that the optimum engine solution for the European Airbus was an optimized RB.207 in the form of the smaller RB.211. However, Mintech's attempts in trying to get the European Airbus partners to adopt an aircraft of three engine design met with failure.

The UK Ministry's actions took place under Benn's stewardship and perhaps reflect Benn's early bias for an American RB.211 deal, which would ultimately converge with Lockheed on the L1011, and his apparent willingness to sabotage Rolls-Royce's development of its large 60,000 lbst RB.207 high by-pass turbofan engine, on which the 'Jumbo Twin' and Airbus concepts depended.

Commercial Aviation Imperatives

In the UK, Hawker Siddeley was well aware from past experience how to design and develop aircraft. By teaming up with the French and the West Germans in Europe, they collectively produced designs which addressed market needs, and which had been identified by proven interrogative methods. Derek Brown of Hawker Siddeley Hatfield wrote of the Airbus experience, reflecting on the competing priorities:

A review of the historical development of the major aircraft characteristics is helpful in the formulation of future requirements since often extrapolations from the past can give a useful indication of where a future requirement may lie. The formulation of requirements for future aircraft may of necessity be a chicken and egg process...

Past history, has shown [advances in the technical state of the art] had a profound effect on the history of transport aircraft development

Brown's astute, and empirically supported, view is very informative and highlights the tensions between international and social influences on aircraft design when considered against forward airline requirements based on state of the art and industry technical ability.

Early European air-bus studies, of large capacity short haul aircraft, were based on the technical developments of wing and HBR technologies under research in the UK. The joint European studies, as well as being technically competent, focused on areas which did not threaten to compete with, or duplicate US projects. The Europeans conceived an aircraft and projected it to operate over short distances, in the European theatre. It was to be an aircraft and engines that matched high cycle usage that would be required by the European operators.

Wing Technology

Hawker Siddeley had been researching and developing a third generation wing, a high cycle wing that was focused for use on the relatively low speeds associated with climbing and landing, where the aircraft would be expected to spend most of its time in a high cycle operation. Similarly, a high cycle engine would be required, one that utilized designs and technologies that focused on the engine's main requirement to spend most of its operating time providing thrust for climbing and landing.

Rolls-Royce and Hawker Siddeley would have worked very closely together to produce the optimum integrated powerplant package and aft loaded wing that addressed the European criteria for a high capacity, high cycle rate, twin turbofan-powered airbus.

Wing and Engine Integration

Brown's assessment of what type of aircraft would be required by airlines was honed by experience and was supported by advances in the technical state of the art. Hawker Siddeley's innovative aft-loaded wing was a pivotal technology for the European Airbus. Hawker's firmly stood their ground in support of the equally pivotal engine technology, the RB.207.

In early general arrangement drawings of the Airbus A.300 as depicted in *Flight* 16 February 1967 through to 23 November 1967, all diagrams and artists' illustrations showed the A.300 sporting underwing engines with short nacelles.

Between 12 June and 14 June 1967, at the International Hotel, Los Angeles, California, Wilde and Pickerell, the chief and assistant chief of preliminary design at Rolls-Royce presented details of the company's three-shaft turbofan engine to the AIAA commercial aircraft design and operation meeting. In their presentation, they laid out before their audience details of the two three-shaft engines that had been designed by Rolls-Royce.

'The first is the Trent in the 10,000lb static thrust class scheduled to go into service in the projected Fairchild F228. The second is the RB.207 in the 50,000lb thrust class for large medium and long haul aircraft.'

Wilde and Pickerell in their AIAA paper indicated there could be exceptions to the common understanding of short cowl configurations '...interference drag between the pod and the airframe could affect this situation...'

I suggest that Wilde and Pickerell were establishing the technical grounds, the importance of a close working relationship with the airframe/wing, and generally mapping out the reasons for the use of an intermediate or long nacelle in conjunction with the RB.207. After all, the RB.203 Trent, the other engine they presented at the same meeting, also used an intermediate-length nacelle.

The economic advantages that a twin-engine and large-capacity airbus powered by two of Rolls-Royce's large RB.207 high by-pass turbofans would have over a three-engine design were significant. As such, the results of the Europeans' formulation of requirements logically fitted with Kolk's specification for a 'Jumbo Twin'.

Political Interference Denied

Benn, it appears, was unable to counter the technical or commercial operators' arguments for a change in the European airbus' engine configuration. Hawker Siddeley, SUD-Aviation, Deutsche and Rolls-Royce all continued with their twin design concept. In the United States, both Lockheed and McDonnell-Douglas continued their studies.

However, the US airframers concentrated on further developing their respective wide-body designs and, despite Kolk's insight, the airframers were incorporating three smaller-sized high by-pass ratio turbofan engines in the 30,000 lbst range. On 23 June 1967, Rolls-Royce offered Lockheed the RB.211-06 of 33,260 lbst. Seemingly, support was growing in the US for a three-engine airliner capable of trans-continental, medium to long haul operation.

The initial studies by McDonnell Douglas for a Kolk short haul Jumbo with twin RB.207 engines were allowed to lapse. According to some observers, by June 1967 the studies involving McDonnell Douglas and Rolls-Royce had evolved into a three-engine design based on the RB.211. Yet others suggest that it was to be a month after Rolls-Royce had presented Lockheed with the details of the smaller-sized ATE that Rolls-Royce provided McDonnell Douglas with engineering data and commercial information on the RB.211-06, in July 1967.

Perhaps the month-long delay by Rolls-Royce in making a formal presentation of the mid-size ATE RB.211 for the DC-10 is an indication of both Rolls-Royce's and Douglas' persistence with the 'Jumbo Twin'? If so, the Rolls-Royce company position would have been contrary to the emphasis that Benn's Mintech was placing on the UK company to secure an engine supply for a triple-engine aircraft design.

No mention is made by Wilde and Pickerell of a design for a mid-size ATE engine in the 30,000 lb thrust class, and the engine designs presented in early June 1967 appear to support the thinking that the RB.207 would power a Douglas-Kolk 'Jumbo Twin'. Nevertheless, McDonnell Douglas was to abandon its twin-engine design in favour of an aircraft designed around three engines.

Lockheed's Two into Three

Lockheed, as the first to receive details of the 30,000 lb thrust class RB.211, may have been instrumental in mustering the support of US airlines for a three-engine aircraft design. Lockheed's proposal possibly encouraged enough support from the US airlines to cause Douglas to adopt a similar three-engine design. Lockheed also, arguably, promoted their design in the full knowledge that it was contrary to Kolk's specification.

Such a position effectively meant that Lockheed was dictating terms to Kolk, and to American Airlines. However, Hayward suggests that Lockheed, and its L1011, was 'Rolls' primary target', and seemingly Benn's emphasis on pushing Rolls-Royce into a US tri-jet appears to give support to that view.

Critically, the most important political criteria for Rolls-Royce in its bid to secure financial funding from the UK Labour government, in the form of Launch Aid for its family of ATE high bypass aero-engines, was the emphatic stipulation that Benn placed on Rolls-Royce being able to secure a US outlet for the RB.211. Rolls-Royce appeared to have been led into the RB.211 development of its ATE design as a condition of Launch Aid.

Was Rolls-Royce going to receive Launch Aid for both a mid-size engine for the US market and the larger RB.207 for the European market? Or perhaps Rolls-Royce was persuaded that the cost of development and production of a successful mid-size RB.211 would provide the funding for the larger RB.207?

Despite the obstacles, Kolk, McDonnell-Douglas and Rolls-Royce continued to work very closely together and by early 1968, the McDonnell-Douglas board were confident of enough US political support, airline orders and technical engineering solutions to launch their latest airliner, the DC-10.

CHAPTER NINE

AMERICAN LAUNCH THE DC-10

Despite initiating his design requirement at Lockheed, Kolk chose the McDonnell-Douglas aircraft in preference to the competing Lockheed L1011. Some observers have suggested that Kolk deliberately snubbed the Lockheed L1011 because of Lockheed's emphasis on promoting a three-engine aircraft instead of Kolk's original requirement for a twin.

However, Kolk's decision is significant because even though Lockheed's product was judged by airlines in general to have been a superior design, Kolk was probably persuaded that the DC-10 would have a superior operating edge because of McDonnell Douglas's substantial presence, through the DC-8 and the DC-9, in the commercial jet aircraft market. Lockheed, by comparison, had a small commercial market presence and, since the Electra, had 'been out of the civil market for more than a decade, and [it had] never yet built a big civil jet'. Lockheed's biggest problem with the airlines was credibility.

The Lockheed Corporation was in serious financial troubles and budgeted costs were heavily over-running on three very large US military projects for McNamara's Department of Defense. Lockheed was faced with serious financial penalties, for instance, for failing to meet the total procurement package contract conditions associated with the C5A. Because of its inability to deal with the technical problems, Lockheed was unable to deliver the C5A aircraft to the USAF and therefore it was unable to receive payment and to generate a positive cash flow from the program. Lockheed was cash strapped and together with its lack of credibility for commercial jet activity, these were good reasons for Kolk and Rolls-Royce to back McDonnell-Douglas and the DC-10.

Perhaps Kolk was a bit more than suspicious of Lockheed's circumstances and perhaps also wary of McNamara's true intentions? Perhaps Kolk likened McNamara's utilization of Lockheed and the C5A to Trippe and Boeing – the control of the supply of large aircraft to the commercial airlines.

Lockheed were not in a strong enough position financially or commercially, unlike McDonnell Douglas, to compete in the airline industry. Mr James S. McDonnell, probably offering a similar argument to that used by Robert McNamara to reduce duplication, approached the then-governor of California, Mr Ronald Reagan, to enlist his support to close the Lockheed L1011 project but 'Old Mac' was gently rebuffed. Un-deterred, 'Old Mac' authorised the go ahead on the DC-10.

On 19 February 1968, in what was supposed to be a knock-out blow to the competing Lockheed L1011 aircraft, Mr George A. Spater, then the president of American Airlines, and Mr James S. McDonnell of McDonnell-Douglas announced American Airlines' intention to acquire the McDonnell-Douglas DC-10. This was a shock to Lockheed and there was general agreement within the US aviation industry that American Airlines had left its competitors at the starting gate.

Normally, such a fatal commercial blow would have been enough to persuade the competition to quit. Even though Lockheed were supposed to be out of the game, Haughton stubbornly refused to give in and was busy making moves behind the scenes in a bid to re-inflate the stricken L1011 project.

Rolls-Royce Almost Succeeds

Together with American Airlines' decision to announce the DC-10 order, it was also reported in the US aviation press that American Airlines had declared its intention to have the British Rolls-Royce RB.211 High By-pass Ratio turbofan aero-engine on its aircraft. In what appears to have been a calculated snub to both Lockheed and McNamara, American Airlines had chosen the DC-10 to be powered by the RB.211.

Interestingly, Rene Francillon in his history of McDonnell-Douglas aircraft makes no mention of American's preference of the Rolls-Royce RB.211 for their original DC-10 order.

The Rolls-Royce RB.211 engine was to have powered American Airlines' initial order for twenty-five DC-10s and twenty-five options. All together, American 'declared [an] interest of up to 100 [DC-10s] by 1975'.

The American Airlines options were covered by a non-refundable deposit and with such a cast-iron commitment the DC-10's future looked to be both formidable and assured. McDonnell-Douglas and American were very confident of the one additional order required to launch production.

The import into the US of the British Rolls-Royce engine had been tentatively approved by the US Treasury, on the condition that the British government's state-owned airline

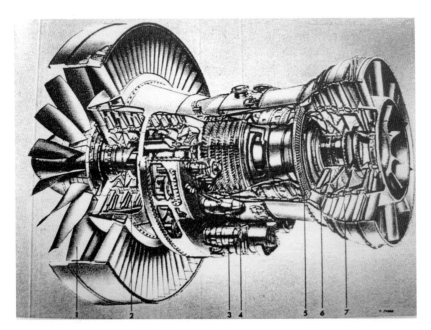

An early general arrangement diagram of the RB.211-06. (Rolls-Royce)

British European Airways would order an American trijet with Rolls-Royce engines. In February 1968, *Flight* reported: 'According to *Aviation Daily*, the US Treasury has approved the choice of foreign engine on the "understanding that BEA will order in due course an American trijet which would also be powered with Rolls-Royce engines".'

Newspaper coverage of the likely deal between American Airlines and its choice of the RB.211 suggested that other US airlines would follow the lead with orders for the same combination, and in significant quantities, effectively securing half the market for the next fifteen years.

Going for Broke

In its bid to gain political support for its ATE engine family, Rolls-Royce, on 29 June 1967, had supplied the UK Ministry of Aviation with a forecast engine sales figure for the period 1970–79. The forecast was based on the hypothesis that there would be only one engine manufacturer and one aircraft manufacturer supplying this market.

It was generally accepted throughout the US aerospace industry that whichever of the competing wide-body designs secured strong launch orders, then that design would be the only one produced. This thinking also underpinned the concept of engine supply for the new aircraft. There would be no duplication – only one engine supplier and one aircraft supplier.

On 29 February 1968, American Airlines announced that they would order the RB.211 for their DC-10s. Understandably, McDonnell-Douglas and Rolls-Royce rightly forecast that as the winners in the tri-jet competition, they would be the only ones to supply the airlines with a wide-body high bypass turbofan trijet.

Rolls-Royce Commit the RB.211 to Development

Such was the Rolls-Royce board's high level of confidence at being awarded the contract to supply RB.211 engines for the McDonnell-Douglas DC-10 that the company had already committed itself by investing substantial amounts of financial and production resources in the RB.211 aero-engine's development in advance of a firm order.

Rolls-Royce tooled up to produce the 06 series of the RB.211. In 1974, John Coplin, Chief Designer RB 211, in an interview with Kenneth Owen recalled: 'Much of the long-lead-time material and designs had to be laid down before we saw the first running result of the 06.'

This was a bold move by Rolls-Royce and perhaps reflected the aggressive management style required of Rolls-Royce by its American customers. It also reinforces the view that the British company was firmly aligned with Kolk and the DC-10.

John Coplin:

This might not have mattered too much if the RB 211 (unlike earlier, smaller engines) had not involved many special-purpose manufacturing machine tools. For the fan casing and other key parts, indeed, special factories were being set up, all tailored to specific designs. The company was tooling up for a high rate of production.

Sources suggest that as much as the equivalent of £60 million was ploughed into the business that, for example, funded forward purchases of large quantities of long lead items and large capital projects. This meant that the consequences of a major design change could be extremely serious. A change would be expensive in both time and money.

In addition to the significant resources allocated to the RB.211, other resources were also being committed by Rolls-Royce to the design and development of RB.203 for the US Fairchild F.228 and the RB.207 for the European Airbus A.300. Such a massive commitment by the company was clearly a very significant financial risk but one where the company had secured substantial airframe programmes for the engines. With the company precariously balanced, any significant technical changes to the ATE engine programme would have drastic consequences for the whole company. In addition, and most peculiarly, Rolls-Royce was going through a number of dramatic changes to its project management processes.

Project Management Changes

Following what appears to have been the politically inspired McKinsey report of 1965, Rolls-Royce had adopted new project management methods and techniques, and perhaps these were more in tune with what was expected by customers in the American markets.

The DTi report of 1973 on the failure of Rolls-Royce Limited:

> The accumulation of design experience is essential to good design ... (in the organisational structure before the RB 211) small groups of junior designers had been managed by more experienced section leaders who specialised in particular areas of engines ... Section leaders had been, in turn, supervised by more senior and experienced men, and the same learning and imparting of experience occurred. The change to the (RB211) project organisation ... tended to break up this process, cutting off the younger men from direct contact with the sources of experience, and eliminating the role of section leader ... Project management fell into the hands of development engineers and the essential independence of the design function was lost.

Over-Reach

Owen, in his 1974 interview with John Coplin, Chief Designer RB.211, was perhaps indicating that a planned design change was known to be in the offing. The circumstances which have been built up in this work so far, together with the threat of changes to the engines, lead me to suggest that within the framework of my hypothesis, this precarious instance indicates the application of over-reach in action. It was the culmination of the forces which would cause Rolls-Royce Limited to reach its tipping point. As we will learn, Rolls-Royce had three engines cancelled: the RB.203 for the US Fairchild F228; the RB.211-06 for the DC-10; and the RB.207 for the Airbus A.300. Then the company was forced to accept changes to the RB.211 and supply it solely for the Lockheed L1011.

Rolls-Royce was being over-reached materially, financially, organisationally and technically. These symptoms, I suggest, were the main indicators of Rolls-Royce's far reaching High By-pass Ratio technology acquisition programme that was the RB.211 for the U.S. market and specifically the Labour-endorsed bid for the Lockheed L1011 aircraft which all together would cause the company to fail.

CHAPTER TEN

PERFIDIOUS LABOUR:
THE MACHINATIONS OF THE MINISTRY MEN

During Rolls-Royce's push to secure orders for the RB.211 in the United States, the British Labour government had afforded Rolls-Royce Limited every-assistance in its bid to secure American business.

Despite Frank Kolk, American Airlines' chief engineer, advocating a preference for the superior economics of a twin, a concept that the Europeans agreed with in the proposed RB.207-powered A.300, Rolls-Royce was steered in its efforts towards supplying the smaller optimized RB.211 engine for a US tri-jet.

In his reply to a question tabled by Mr Maxwell-Hyslop MP, Mr Stonehouse, Minister for Aviation, confirmed the government's support: 'The highest possible support has been provided to Rolls-Royce in its attempt to get the RB211 into the American airbus.'

With no three-engine European airframe in prospect for the RB.211, some considered that Rolls-Royce had no alternative but to make strenuous efforts to get onto a US airframe. Although *Interavia* emphasized the transatlantic aspect of the RB.211, in the European context the RB.207 was being developed for the twin A.300 Airbus and the RB.203 was being proposed for various Hawker Siddeley feederliner projects.

Political Un-certainty

However, according to *The Economist*, serious political storm clouds had been gathering around the transatlantic aviation scene for some time:

What Mr Wilson has done is to make it difficult, some might think it impossible, for one of the biggest domestic airlines in the United States - American Airlines- to buy Rolls-Royce engines. And as American decides, so goes at least half the market for big, short range jets during the next fifteen years. On Monday American decided on its aircraft, the 252 seat DC-10, but left open the question of what engines are going into them. The order, 25 aircraft by 1973, and another 25 in 1973, is worth with its engines close on £350 million. There are only two engine companies still in the running American General Electric and British Rolls-Royce. On design ability, production expertise, price reputation and past ability to deliver the goods - in short every feature that counts with airlines - Rolls-Royce has the edge over General Electric. Except one: it is British.

The Economist concluded by repeating the US Treasury's position that the British Labour government could still influence the deal: 'The balance might conceivably still be swung by authorising British European Airways to buy one of the American jets and specifying that it will be Rolls-Royce powered.'

The US Treasury's conditional approval for the supply of the RB.211 in return for a reciprocal trade deal could not be met by Rolls-Royce Limited but it could be met by the political paymasters of British European Airways (BEA), the Wilson Labour government. Intriguingly, despite the McDonnell Douglas DC-10 needing just one more order to commit the aircraft to production and therefore secure the engine order for Rolls-Royce, no order for the DC-10 was placed by BEA and neither, it seems, was BEA given authorisation to commit to the DC-10. Yet at a later date, BEA would order the Rolls-Royce powered Lockheed L1011.

The Rolls-Royce RB.211 engine, sporting the features which counted most with the airlines, was best placed to secure significant business with American airlines, and as Benn was very keen to emphasize, Rolls-Royce would do so in the world's largest and most lucrative commercial airliner market. But, according to *The Economist*, the Wilson Labour government was clearly out of favour with the US administration.

The very fragile condition of the UK economy in late 1967 meant that the Wilson government desperately needed a strategy to politically re-engage with the US administration so that the US would look more favourably on a Labour request for IMF financial assistance. The UK economy was said to be in a parlous state and the Labour government was in dire need of financial assistance from the IMF.

Wilson's Labour government had caused a considerable amount of political controversy with the Americans and the US was in no mood to allow Britain's Rolls-Royce to secure major contracts with US airlines at the expense of American industry. While Rolls-Royce was busy securing business for its RB.211, *The Economist* chipped in to remind its readers of the terrible fate that could befall the UK company: 'How closed the American market itself will become as a result of the F-111 cancellation is a matter for horrid speculation… The Buy American act will be back in full force.'

It appears that *The Economist* could see, perhaps from a vantage point, the air of political turbulence that lay in waiting for Rolls-Royce. US political relations with the UK had cooled after Wilson cancelled the purchase of US F-111 bombers which were meant for the RAF. Wilson's action was but one response to the massive cuts which the Labour government had to make to reduce the UK Treasury's budgets.

The warning by *The Economist* in late January 1968 appears to address the tense political relations between the US and the UK. However, the cancellation of a relatively small order for a US military aircraft was not going to cause the US company to close its doors. The impact of the cancellation would hardly have been felt, unlike the dreadful consequences for UK companies that were meted out when Healey and Jenkins between them cancelled the TSR.2, the HS.681 and the P.1154.

The article in *The Economist* provides an insight into the complexities that could be expected of the negotiations at the sovereign state level to supply British strategic technology to an economically challenged US administration. Technically, it could be argued that the British engine was ahead of its US competitor but politically, the path was fraught with vagaries.

The article also provides evidence that US economic considerations were going to be foremost among the controlling factors of any US-UK trade decision. The article's publication in January came just weeks before American Airlines was to announce the selection of the DC-10 powered by the Rolls-Royce engine.

Benn and Concorde

One particularly sharp thorn in the flesh of both the UK Labour government and the US administration was the Anglo-French Concorde. The US Treasury was disdainful of the Concorde project being financed with monies from the IMF, and even threatened to withhold IMF funding to the UK if the US suspected that IMF monies would be used by the UK to finance UK aircraft programmes which competed with similar US aircraft. Interestingly, when the UK was initially discussing a supersonic transport, it offered to collaborate with the US but the US refused. However, such an understanding on interdependent competition did not stop the US from borrowing UK ideas and hastily setting up their own similar requirements.

In the UK, the Concorde programme was seen by Labour's anti-aviation ministers as the epitome of the largesse of the public purse seemingly supporting the excesses of the UK aviation industry.

In 1967 Benn, the Labour Minister for Technology, on taking office muttered: 'If only Concorde would crash on the QE2, all my problems would be solved.' (Costello and Hughes 1976)

Without France's agreement, the project could not be stopped; only technical failure could justify a UK withdrawal, and so the anti-Concorde ministers in Wilson's Labour government held on to the hope that Concorde might bring about its own demise through technical failure. (Ponting 1989) By 1968, a series of exacting tests lay ahead of the Concorde prototypes. If the aircraft flight tests proved that there were technical problems, or showed that there was a reason to doubt the safety or the viability of supersonic flight, and that any technical problems would affect the aircraft's commercial viability, then Concorde would be cancelled.

What can be seen from this insight is that Labour tried desperately to cancel Concorde but only succeeded in arousing the suspicions of the French over the Labour government's commitment to a European airbus. Emphasizing Labour's rhetorical commitment to Europe, and despite the findings of the Plowden report, Newhouse honed in on the duplicitous nature of the UK Labour party, a point that would hang over the heads of Benn and Stonehouse when negotiating with their European partners on Airbus. 'The Labour Party was far more comfortable dealing with Americans than with continental Europeans.'

The Minister for Technology, Benn showed no signs of discomfort or disquiet in his handling of Rolls-Royce when he was cajoling them towards a deal on an American air bus.

Writing of the politics of the European A.300, Professor Keith Hayward notes that:

> ... Collaboration was also seen as a means of avoiding an unpalatable degree of dependence upon the United States in a crucial industry; an industry which not only affected a nation's ability to retain a degree of military independence but which also constituted, or so it was believed, a significant technological asset benefiting a nation's overall economic and industrial competitivity [sic].

With the Labour government's push for a RB.211-powered wide-body rather than a RB.207-powered airbus, their politically led technical preference indicated a willingness to subject the UK's crucial industry to be dependent on the US, despite European efforts to counter the dominance of the US aviation industry. The actions of the anti-airbus Labour government and their cajoling of Rolls-Royce to secure US business are, I suggest, clear indicators of political forces used to achieve Rolls-Royce's over-reach scenario.

CHAPTER ELEVEN

AMERICAN LEADS THE WAY

In 1967, *Flight* reported that from a Lockheed aerodynamicist's perspective, the airlines which were interested in the DC-10 favoured the Rolls-Royce RB.211 as its power-plant. It is from such a view point that I suggest that the definitive pre-launch DC-10 was offered to airlines during late 1967 and early 1968, and that by February 1968 the DC-10 was designed around the Rolls-Royce RB.211 power-plant, which would have been supplied in its entirety, including nacelle and pod up to the pylon mountings.

By March 1968, the combination of the American McDonnell-Douglas DC-10 powered by the British Rolls-Royce RB.211 had gained credence and momentum with American Airlines, sufficient enough for the respected aviation journalist Arthur Reed to write in *The Times* of 1 March 1968: 'The company has evidently almost succeeded in beating stiff opposition from General Electric. Rolls-Royce's engine, the R.B.-211, has been judged cheaper to buy and to operate than its American competitor.'

Pratt & Whitney's engine was out of the running and the General Electric offering was projected to be more expensive to buy and to operate. In other words, the technologies available to the US companies were behind the learning curve that Rolls-Royce had already progressed along. The initial US high by-pass technologies were little or no match for Rolls-Royce's third generation ATE high by-pass aero-engine.

In the smaller stakes, the Rolls-Royce RB.203 Trent had been chosen to power the Fairchild F-228 feeder-liner, a US version of the Fokker F.28. The three-shaft ATE turbofan was expected to make serious inroads into the Spey and JT8-type markets. With the threat of three third generation Rolls-Royce engines, the RB.203, the RB.211 and the RB.207, hungry for business in the respective feeder-liner and trans-continental markets, together with the willingness of US airlines to buy the advanced UK-produced engines, the US aero-engine industry saw the writing on the wall.

Presidential Permission

America and American Airlines were getting ready to buy British. However, the proposed purchase of British engines released a strong backlash of US protectionist sentiment especially from those US interests that would not benefit from the importing of an all British-built power-plant.

Despite the engine purchase having apparently received US President Johnson's approval, here still existed concerns within the US aviation industry and the political corridors of Capitol Hill about buying the foreign British engines. Therefore, instead of an official announcement made by American Airlines to order the Rolls-Royce RB.211 engine for the DC-10 being made on the same day, the engine order was delayed.

P&W had lost out in the race to power the DC-10, but both P&W and GE were notable for their lack of initial commitment to supply a total power-plant package. For Douglas in particular, the commitment shown by Rolls-Royce to supply a total power-plant package was of great importance. Douglas, as the authority for its airframe integration, had in part lost its independence as a result of having to compensate the airlines for the technical and performance inadequacies of equipment supplied on the DC-8. It was a salutary lesson for Douglas and the US company employed the lessons learned in its apportioning of work-share and responsibilities on the DC-10. For the new McDonnell-Douglas project, the equipment and engine makers would have to stand by their word on the performance of the total power-plant package or pay the contracted consequences on performance related shortfalls. McDonnell-Douglas's actions in this instance mirrored those of the procurement mechanism masterminded by the US Secretary of Defense Robert McNamara.

Total Package Procurement (TPP)

US Secretary of Defense Robert McNamara was responsible for the introduction of a new type of contract that significantly affected the relationship between the US administration and the Military Industrial Complex. The application of the new style of contract was designed to bring about a significant change in the procurement relationship.

A *Flight* correspondent wrote:

> Since World War II neither the executive branch of the US Government, nor the Congress, have been satisfied with the administration of defence contracts. Virtually every US Secretary of Defense has wrestled with these problems, but credit for the most concrete results so far achieved clearly is going to go to Robert S McNamara, the present Secretary of Defense.

The total package procurement concept was introduced by McNamara for the Department of Defense procurement agencies to heighten the intensity of military competitions.

As Boyne noted:

> 'Total Package Procurement' (TPP), the new concept required manufacturers to compete for an entire program, from research and development through production, all under a single contract. Standards were to be set for price, schedule and performance, and it was made well known that the government did not intend to budge from the agreements ... A clause stipulated that the contractor was responsible for the complete system performance, including engines, and was required to take action to correct any discrepancies.

One of the first of the new type of contracts, known as the total procurement price contract, was awarded to Lockheed when in 1965 McNamara chose the Lockheed aircraft design to fulfil the USAF's CX-HLS requirement.

Lockheed was to experience many problems with the design, development and production of the C5A (CX-HLS) strategic aircraft, which stemmed from the contract:

> ... the contract; both hoped that it would be possible to execute. Yet the contract was an unfulfillable monstrosity that worked against the interest of the government and the contractor with almost equal ferocity. Few will be surprised to learn that it originated in the office of the Secretary of Defense. (Boyne 1998)

Another US company that was awarded a total procurement price contract was General Electric Corporation. Secretary of Defense Robert McNamara on 25 August 1965 awarded GE the $459 million contract, GE's single biggest award in its history, to develop and build the high by-pass ratio technology TF39-GE-1 aero-engine to power the first fifty-eight examples of the Lockheed C-5A aircraft.

> As a rule, designing and building a new engine takes more time than the same process for an airframe. The engine ... serves as the very heart of the airplane ... Therefore, even though the General Electric total-package procurement contract (AF33-657-15003) closely resembled one awarded Lockheed for the airframe, the Air Force handled the two differently. (Knaack 1998)

Knaack noted that: 'The [US] Air Force played a more active part in development of the engine for the C–5A.' At least one overt part that the USAF played in the development of the TF39 was to receive the bare engines from GE and then to deliver the same to Lockheed. Perhaps this was done to minimise collusion between Lockheed and the General Electric companies in the event of expected cost over-runs.

McNamara's TPP, the procurement process and its ultimate political aim of repositioning the power away from the US military industrial complex towards the White House would also involve and affect its interdependent allies across the Atlantic. It would no doubt have an impressive effect on the procurement processes and the manner in which the UK Labour government would engage the UK aviation industry as the Labour government set about its demise.

The official roll-out of the C5. (RAeS)

CHAPTER TWELVE

DUPLICATION AND INTERDEPENDENCE, OR DUPLICITY AND DEPENDENCY?

Were the Wilson Labour government and US administration working together towards promoting healthy competition between their respective aviation industry champions as the motives for the Plowden Report alluded to, or were the US and UK governments looking to reduce the number of aero-engine manufacturers and leave the UK reliant on the US for its prime movers?

It appears highly probable that Rolls-Royce, perhaps taking its cue from the Labour government, had formulated its strategies for achieving significant US aero-engine business so as to take advantage of McNamara's political objectives. McNamara's manoeuvrings, which were made in relation to the US aviation industry but which also reverberated across the Atlantic, focused on how to reposition the balance of power away from the American military industrial complex and to re-invest that power in the White House. A key concept policy that enabled McNamara to work towards his aims was formulated on his concern with avoiding or reducing un-necessary duplication. His preferred instrument for pushing through the changes, which he saw as necessary, was the Total Procurement Price contract.

Interdependence

In the UK, a key post-war foreign policy that had been promoted by successive UK governments in their dealings with the US *vis-à-vis* geo-political security and trade was supported by the political idea of interdependence.

In November 1962, the technical editor of *Flight* wrote on interdependence and how to avoid duplication between friends. During the meeting between Mr Thorneycroft and Mr McNamara they would have discussed the principle of interdependence at some length, whereby each nation would assist the other in developing something of outstanding military value. Britain's key technological skill was in its advanced vertical take-off aircraft, the Hawker Siddeley HS.1154 and the Bristol Siddeley engine the BS.100. However, the technical editor pointed out that 'if America runs true to form, she will be at present engaged in hastily trying to initiate her own programmes in such fields ... unofficial reports describe the haste with which American requirements for lift units [aero-engines] ... are being formulated ...'

It appears that rather than allow healthy competition between the two interdependent, nations the UK would allow the US to view its advanced aviation technologies, take them, hastily generate a need for them, and implement them for its own use.

Lloyd, in his review of the Ministry of Aviation upon its incorporation into Mintech, wrote that, 'Increasing cost of aeronautical projects ... led to the idea of collaboration between governments in joint developments ... with the United States of America under the heading of "Interdependence" ...'

With the election of the Labour party to government in 1964, the US found it had either a willing accomplice or at least an attentive listener towards the aims of US strategic interests. The Wilson Labour government in 1964, and later through the Ministry of Technology under Wedgwood Benn, was ideologically determined and politically committed to repositioning the British aviation industry. In November 1965,

> According to *The Sunday Times* the British aircraft industry is to be axed and dismembered by the new Government on the strength of a report by Mr Richard Worcester, an ex-journalist aviation consultant. Mr Worcester was the author of a 1956 report, *An Industry Gone Mad*, which argued that subsonic jets were not needed.

The United States aviation industry's political and industrial interests must have been rubbing their hands in glee at the prospect of Labour's attack on the UK aviation industry. The demise of the UK's manufacturing aviation industry could ultimately mean one less technically competent competitor and the addition of the UK's defence and commercial markets, ripe for US exploitation.

Plowden

As soon as Labour got into office, they hastily initiated committees to report on their targets. The British aircraft industry would be the subject of the Plowden Committee, which held its first session on 11 January 1965. A core theme continued by the Plowden report was that of interdependence and strategic co-operation. However, the Plowden report, far from recommending the UK aviation industry co-operate with the US, instead emphasized it must collaborate with its European partners.

The production of the Plowden report was overshadowed by the 'wet nurse' statement made by Mr Denis Healey, Minister for Defence, on 8 January 1966 to the air correspondent of *The Daily Telegraph*. Healey had let his political face mask slip and out popped his unadulterated bias against the UK aviation industry.

While the Plowden Committee were forging ahead, Kenneth Owen reported on the 'widespread concern in the aircraft industry arising from the danger of cancellation of military projects and negotiations now proceeding and about to be concluded on the purchase terms of alternative aircraft from the United States'. Owen emphasized the core danger lurking behind the minister's mask and the threat the then-Labour government posed to the British aircraft industry by repeating Mr Healey's phrase that the minister pejoratively spat out when he referred to the UK industry. Healey likened his dealings with the UK aviation industry interests to: 'Wet-nursing mentally retarded children.'

Healey's language suggests that the Labour government's intentions towards the UK aircraft industry were prejudiced and biased, with a base of *a priori* intent, which therefore, arguably, influenced the Labour government's underlying remit of the Plowden Committee and, as it appears, the pre-determined conclusion that Wilson wanted to be drawn from the report.

The Plowden Report judged that the US industry was three times more productive than Britain's. Based on this spurious claim, the Labour government cancelled three British projects: the supersonic VSTOL P.1154; the strategic STOL transport HS.681; and, later, the TSR.2. These aircraft were cancelled because, according to Solly Zuckerman and in the minds of the Labour ministers, the aircraft would not be delivered on time. Instead, the Labour government ordered the destruction of the UK projects' prototypes so there could be no duplicated effort and decided to import foreign US products as replacements, in the case of the TSR2, the General Dynamics F-111. The British industry's reaction to the cuts was recorded on 11 February 1965, with Hawker Siddeley announcing at 6 p.m. that 14,000 men out of 40,000 would be made redundant.

Despite the spurious claims made by Labour, the organised demise of the UK aviation industry was further underscored when on 18 February 1965, *Flight* reported on the Anglo-US agreements between Secretary for State for Defence Mr Healey and the US Defense Secretary Mr McNamara. In a written parliamentary reply on 11 February 1965, details were given of the 'agreements signed between Britain and the USA for the purchase and "co-production" of US military aircraft'. Britain, it seemed, was not up to the immediate challenges, according to the Labour government ministers, of producing its own aircraft and instead in the future would have to rely on foreign imports. In the short term the industry was in turmoil, unable to secure long term financial or political support for UK projects.

Some eighteen months later, Adrian Lombard, the Rolls-Royce director of engineering, in his address to the Royal Society in June 1966 commented on the effects of the Plowden Committee on the UK aviation industry: 'The enquiry into the aircraft industry by the Plowden Committee created a background of uncertainty that had its effect upon long term policy.'

The onset of long-term uncertainty was aided and abetted by the uncertainty of UK government support for the UK aviation industry. The precarious positions that aviation manufacturers sometimes found themselves in were, it seems, the result of ministerial machinations.

In the DTi report that reviewed the collapse of Rolls-Royce, the authors highlighted a part of the Plowden Report and drew their readers' attention to the vulnerability of the aviation industry:

Advances in technology have made life particularly difficult for suppliers of aircraft. The development costs of military projects are usually borne entirely by the customer but the manufacturer's resources are tied up in fewer and increasingly expensive types; he is highly vulnerable if one is suddenly cancelled. On civil projects the manufacturer himself normally finds at least half, sometimes more, of the development costs. He aims to recover this money over a range of sales. If these fail to mature because some unexpected technical advance gives an advantage to a competitive aircraft he bears heavy losses. (part paragraph 37)

I suggest that the vulnerability that Lombard was referring to was the long term uncertainty and confusion which were promoted by the Labour-inspired findings of the Plowden Report. In addition, I suggest that Lombard understood the reach and the complexity of the Labour government, and these points are those which MacCrindle and Godfrey allude to in paragraph 37 of their report into the collapse of Rolls-Royce Limited.

Benn and the Train Robbers

The confusion in the UK industry, arguably, was exactly what Labour intended to achieve through the Plowden Report. Beyond creating long term uncertainty and vulnerability, there was the prospect that the industry would self-destruct, suffocating under the pillow of Labour's cosseted inactivity. Wilson and Benn were strategically placed to push for change in the UK aircraft industry, which Benn in his anti-aviation tones pejoratively likened to the 'train robbers'. Benn was in a position to dictate the terms of financial assistance or Launch Aid the UK government would offer Rolls-Royce. He would also be in a position to dictate the sales terms which would allow Rolls-Royce to qualify for increased support. Benn would also be in a position to exact his will on an industry he considered to be no better than the base criminals who had committed the Great Train Robbery, an event at the time which outraged the decent British public.

Benn's anti-aviation prejudice was as consistent as it was ill-informed. *Flight*, July 1967, reported on the after-dinner differences between the president of the SBAC, Mr R. F. Hunt and Mr Benn, the new minister for technology responsible for aviation; Mr Hunt rebuked Benn's distorted view of the industry's successes: '… it comes as a surprise that a Minister of the Crown still sees fit to criticise the industry's achievements …'

Echoing the industry's view of the Minister, the respected industry journal *Engineering* reported on Benn's accession as head of the Ministry of Technology in 1967. The article sought to understand Benn's position relative to the long term future of the UK industry, all the more so as Benn was one of the chief architects of Labour's policies towards the UK aviation industry, and it was the Labour government that had allowed the indicated the state of affairs to develop. *Engineering* commented on the precarious state of affairs:

> And this at a moment in Britain's history when it is no exaggeration to say that technological success has the chance to save the country economically and internationally, and technological failure would certainly contribute to a Britain bereft of power and influence in the world.

The article in *Engineering* referred to Benn as a dedicated politician but, interestingly, one whose intentions were unclear and because he was unclear then it was a particular concern for the UK aviation industry:

> The dedicated politician is difficult to pin down, his decisions and motives difficult to analyze. In an interview with the Minister it was for example, difficult to draw him out on the vital question of Anglo-American relations in technology. Yet because one knows [Benn] is so capable in grasping all the ramifications of his developing function, because he is so vitally interested in the regeneration of Britain, because he impresses with his

sheer competence, one is more than ordinarily concerned if he appears to have doubt or reticence.

Benn sowed doubt and confusion by refusing to commit to any clear and focused long term plans for the British aviation industry. To add even more to the state of confusion, Benn, the new minister for technology, changed the focus of the collaborative plan, and instead of the UK industry focussing on Europe Benn saw 'Britain building a bridge between Europe and the United States'. But perhaps from the *Engineering* readership's point of view, they were not going to be hood-winked and Benn's actions would be dulled by the likelihood of 'socialist interference'. Benn, on the surface, when he was not voicing his prejudices, appeared to project an image of a committed technocrat, but it seems within his office that all he wanted was for the technologies to fail spectacularly so as to gain public sympathy for his intentions and only then would all his problems be solved.

In 1967, Benn's Mintech completed the planned absorption of the Ministry of Aviation. John Stonehouse, the pro-European Minister for Aviation who had laboured to get a deal together between Britain, France and West Germany, now found that his new boss had, yet again, shifted the political goal posts.

Hayward recorded Stonehouse's view:

> The prejudices against the (Airbus) and European collaboration amongst British Ministers was really quite extraordinary. It was only by a very narrow majority in the Cabinet committee that it was agreed that I should go to the meeting to begin negotiations. My colleagues were always tying us up and saying that they were not going to finance it unless a market was established.

Peter Lloyd, director-general of engine research and development at the Ministry of Technology, in a review of his time at the Ministry of Aviation summed up the context surrounding the politically motivated changes within the aviation industry:

> Another substantial change during this period [1959-1967] has been in the public image of the aircraft industry and of the responsible Department of State. The enthusiasm of the post war decade has changed to disillusionment over the high cost of maintaining the aircraft industry and it was against this background that the Plowden Committee made its investigation of the industry's problems.

It is uncertain whose enthusiasm changed and to what extent there was shared disillusionment, for example among the British public, but uncertainty was Labour's chief ally. Labour instigated the Plowden investigation, yet pre-empted the report's conclusions by homing in on those aspects of the report which fitted in with Labour's plans to dismantle the UK aviation industry. It appears that Labour's jump start investigation pejoratively determined, through the UK press, the British public's image of the UK aviation industry.

In Plowden's first public comment on his committee's investigation into the UK aircraft industry, he indicated that the conclusions that the Labour government were drawing were premature: 'Two more months would have doubled our thinking time.'

However, there is a need to set this statement against his view that there was no 'inherent reason' why Britain should continue to have a 'large aircraft' industry. It might

have been argued that Britain's reason for continuing to have a large aircraft industry was its empirical command of the technologies. However, such was the 'spirit' in which the Plowden committee began their inquiry, and the evidence that they collected led them to firmly believe that Britain should continue to have a substantial aircraft industry. Thus for some of the report's audiences, there might have been a case for believing that a small aircraft produced in substantial numbers would be a suitable reason for allowing the UK aviation industry to continue.

The three main conclusions of the Plowden Report were that there should continue to be a substantial aircraft industry, that it should no longer attempt to cover the whole field and that it should in the fullest possible way co-operate with other European countries. Hayward was to write of the allure of the American market which could not be denied, even though collaboration with the US was a poor choice.

The assumptions which informed the Wilson Labour government's initiation of the Plowden report, of using comparisons between the US and UK aviation industries' manufacturing abilities, economics and production efficiency levels and of government financial support, continued the themes of interdependency and duplication. The published report by Plowden obviously endorsed Labour's position relative to the UK aviation industry, despite the underlying questionable assumptions. The report's questionable endorsement in turn fed support for the Wilson Labour government's negative policies towards the UK aviation industry. It can be argued that the Plowden report was a self-fulfilling prophecy, in that it used as its argument a position of reasoning to counter the authority of inherent and innate reasons, but the reasoning of which was flawed because the spirit into which the Plowden report entered into its study was scientifically and empirically destitute.

One has to ask the question whether Labour were committed to Europe and, as Newhouse asserts, '… Labour didn't share the Conservative Party's faith in Europe as the political answer for Britain.'

Another questionable assumption was the alleged poor performance of the UK aviation industry over the post-war years when placed in comparison with the performance of the equivalent US aviation industry. This argument was cross examined by Max Nibloe in his article 'Performance and Prospects' published by *Interavia* in 1970:

> Alleged poor performance … may prove to be one more of those statements which have come to be accepted as factually accurate simply because they have been repeated so many times and never seriously challenged. Whereas the British performance has been studded with failures, the US performance has had nothing but scintillating success according to popular belief.

Nibloe jibbed at Labour's spurious arguments, which they used against the UK aviation industry. What Benn and his Labour colleagues would not want the British public to focus on was that the US aviation industry is littered with failures of all shapes and hues. As has already been noted, the politically inspired McNamara failed to stop the commercially led Trippe and his powerful push to establish the Boeing 747 and the consequent staving-off of the near disastrous collapse of Boeing, which for the period has to be a defining moment in the history of US aviation.

Hurdling Towards Fate

Mintech set the height of the economic hurdles that Rolls-Royce would have to achieve and thereby gain the Minister's approval for government assistance in the form of Launch Aid. It was in the circumstances of tall economic requirements that the UK Labour government forced Rolls-Royce to focus its commercial future on the US market. Rolls-Royce was steered towards its US direction, aided by the politics of interdependence, and financially it was to be dependent on UK government Launch Aid for developing its high by-pass ratio aero-engine technology. Although the RB.203 Trent had been developed within house, using Rolls-Royce's own company funding, Benn stipulated that UK government Launch Aid would only be available for the RB.211 if that engine in turn would become exclusively dependent on a US airframe manufacturer.

The UK aviation industry was not the only target of Plowden's report. The Plowden report also highlighted the necessity with which the UK government had to improve the way it handled the UK aircraft industry:

> I cannot convey to your Lordships how often and to what depressing effect the weaknesses of government or the government machine were revealed to us in evidence: vacillation, delay and bureaucratic control have left a deep mark.

Nevertheless, the Plowden Report was produced at the Labour government's insistence in a bid to further reposition the UK aviation industry. One of the key levers used against the UK aircraft industry was the significantly greater level of economic support that the UK aviation industry received, in the form of tariff protection, and that this was more than most engineering and precision instrument making industries. Yet Plowden admitted it was pointless to try to be precise in drawing comparisons with other comparable industries, because no other industry was comparable to the aircraft industry. Yet Labour were determined to downplay the significance of the UK aviation industry and treat it as though it was as unimportant as any other non-strategic industry and in the process justify, at least in Labour politicians' minds, the withdrawing of government support or protection.

At the 1968 SBAC Farnborough SLAET lecture, Mallalieu, the Minister of State, Mintech said:

> A further Plowden committee recommendation was that government policy should aim at assisting the industry to become fully competitive and at creating conditions in which it could thrive with no more support or protection than is given to comparable industries.

These words must be tempered with his acknowledgement of the special relationship between the aircraft industry and government:

> ... It is generally realised that this industry, as in other countries, has a very close relationship with the government, certainly much closer than most other engineering industries: but perhaps the full extent of this relationship is not always fully appreciated.

In the United States it was openly acknowledged that the aviation industry was incomparable with any other industry. As Jackson McGowen of McDonnell-Douglas admitted, 'We're neither free enterprise nor Government agencies.'

This critical distinction is a point echoed by Lawrence and Thornton: 'An important source of employment, revenue and prestige, governments look to aerospace, in both its military and commercial dimensions, to place and maintain their countries among the world's most powerful.'

Hayward argues that: '... the aerospace industries are necessarily closely related to vital political and strategic interests of [Nation] states.'

Rather than being an ordinarily comparable industry, Lawrence and Thornton stress the uniqueness of the aerospace industry: 'The intensive and mutually conditioning involvement of [the sovereign] state throughout the entire history of aeronautics has made it into what is arguably the world's most politicized industry.'

The Wilson government had by design allowed an illogical and unjustified comparison of the UK aviation industry, a highly politicised and strategically vital asset, with that of alien states. The consequences of that comparison were to subjugate the UK aviation industry to the US and to allow a significant US industry position to enter into the United Kingdom, with a degree of political and strategic reliance afforded it by the UK government that was greater than had previously been permitted. The increased degree of strategic reliance was obviously at the expense of the indigenous UK industry, an industry that was seen as politically and strategically vital.

This, in my mind, indicates that the Labour government, together with the US administration, conspired politically to undermine the sovereign UK aviation industry, and therefore any positions of technological strength were to be negotiated away by the Labour government to US interests in return for a US agreement towards IMF financial support.

In support of this argument I refer to Hayward, who quoted Henry Nau, who argued against 'normative transnationalism': a belief that economic interdependency impels political interdependency. Whereas Raj Roy argues that economic interdependency goes hand in hand with political interdependency.

Perhaps because of a lack of political mass, the UK Labour politicians were unable to match their transatlantic counterparts in finance, productivity, delivery and were thus behind the Americans' learning curve. Blighted by economic impediments and weaknesses, the Labour government sought inter-dependent shelter from the US. From such a perspective, it seems highly probable that Wilson had indeed sold his soul, and the British nation's soul, in a Faustian pact with the US.

CHAPTER THIRTEEN

THE SCIENCE BEHIND THE ATE DESIGN

L. G. Dawson, chief engineer (projects) Rolls-Royce Ltd., wrote an article entitled 'Engines for Advanced Subsonic Transports'. The article was published on 7 January 1965, by *Flight International*.

Dawson identified that a more effective measurement of propulsive efficiency should take account of engine pod drag:

$$\text{Effective propulsive efficiency} = \frac{\text{Froude Efficiency } \{1 - \text{Pod Drag}\}}{\text{Thrust}}$$

Fundamentally, the number representing thrust over intake momentum drag is of more importance than the by-pass ratio in deciding the propulsive efficiency. Advances in pod aero-dynamics have made the passing of the greater airflow possible without a proportional increase in pod drag, even though the intake is larger in relation to the maximum cross-section area of the pod.

This was the scientific theory that was used as a basis to inform the aero-dynamicists of the benefits of the various nacelle/pod cowling configurations for the new high by-pass ratio turbofan technology.

The result of their scientific investigations would appear in the RB.203 nacelle and pod that was displayed at the Paris Airshow in June 1967.

The Trent nacelle incorporated the gearbox accessories and, together with the engine pod, was structurally integrated with and attached directly onto the engine. The application of scientific theory allowed Rolls-Royce to produce a fully integrated power-plant that underlined Rolls-Royce's confidence when it contractually agreed performance objectives with the US Fairchild aircraft manufacturer.

Reiterating the importance of installation drag and co-operation with aircraft designers, Blunt and Lupton wrote: 'It is clear that installation drag is of paramount importance and that considerable scope exists for co-operative ingenuity on the part of the aircraft and engine designers in achieving the best combination.'

Blunt and Lupton's work directly followed on from earlier work established by Dawson of Rolls-Royce in 1965, and highlighted by Lombard in his address to the Royal Society in 1966.

Landamore of Bristol Siddeley, an advocate of the short cowl in his reference to nacelle design, highlighted that although a short-chord cowl does not suffer the internal losses that affect the long by-pass duct, and although it does benefit from lower nacelle drag, 'There is, however, an additional "scrubbing" drag due to the by-pass flow exhausting over the cowled gas generator at higher-than-flight speed.'

As Landamore pointed out, the problem with the short cowl is the scrubbing of the cold air exiting over the engine core pod. In contrast to Landamore's point, Dawson of Rolls-Royce illustrated a key design feature in a by-pass cycle that would improve aero-dynamic performance. He wrote in *Flight*:

> At higher by-pass ratios it has become possible to hide the auxiliaries in the by-pass duct. In this way, a pod for a by-pass ratio of between two and three is no bigger in diameter than one which would have been required for a by-pass ratio of one in the past.

The key to Dawson's work was to eliminate the external scrubbing and to convert the energy, using an aero-dynamic gear, into internal slow moving air that increased thrust on exit at the turbine planar. This was one of the unique features of the Rolls-Royce family of advanced technology engines and was incorporated in the nacelle of the RB.203, the RB.207 and the RB.211, as was clearly stated by Thompson and Smith: 'The overall result is that even though the three quarter cowl nacelle weighs more than a minimum length cowl and inlet configuration, the performance is sufficiently better than that of the short cowl to overbalance the weight increment.'

The Rolls-Royce aero-dynamic duct technology was initially unique to the Rolls-Royce ATE aero-engines.

Design Centre

Rolls-Royce carried out, in house at Hucknall, the design and testing of all nacelles and cowlings for its power-plants. Of particular importance, Hucknall designed the nacelles and pods for the ATE series, which included the RB.207, the RB.211 and its smaller family member, the RB.203 Trent. In April 1968, *Aircraft Engineering* noted:

> The design of cowlings, intakes and thrust reversers is undertaken by the Rolls-Royce Hucknall design department which has been specialising in this work since 1955. Long and short cowlings for the RB.211 can be provided to suit the preference of the aircraft manufacturer.

Rolls-Royce's previous experience of supplying power-plants to Boeing, in addition to the publicly known tensions between Lockheed and General Electric on the C5A, necessitated that the company, from the outset, would be responsible for and would control all aspects of its revolutionary triple-spool high by-pass ratio advanced technology engine. This included the intellectual property rights for the design of the air intake and the nacelle technologies which it was developing for wide-body and feeder-liner airframes.

Informing the design of the high by-pass ratio power-plant was a new degree of closer cooperation that was taking place between the aero-engine manufacturer and the airframe companies. This closer co-operation was promoted in the design and development of the RB.203 for the HS.136 feeder-liner, the RB.207 for the European Airbus A.300 and the RB.211 for the BAC 2-11. Eltis and Wilde:

> Since by-pass ratio and the chosen ratio of airflow to thrust influence nacelle size, airbleed losses, etc., there is an interrelationship between the choice of engine cycle, power plant and aircraft characteristics which requires the closest consultation between the aircraft designer and the designer of the propulsion system.

Eltis and Wilde as Rolls-Royce design engineers highlighted their awareness of the concerns of the airframe engineers:

> There are also the additional factors f [the effect of fan cowl external drag] and g [the power plant nacelle/aircraft wing or body interference effect] which depend upon the installation and the relation of the engine to the aircraft. These losses are influenced by the design of the pylon and wing and are therefore the responsibility of the airframe constructor.

An interesting feature of the talks that occurred between Lombard and Sutter was the stark lack of co-operation Sutter displayed towards Rolls-Royce. This feature lies in bleak contrast to the close co-operation, for example, that was developed between Rolls-Royce and Hawker Siddeley designers and engineers.

Hawker Siddeley's deputy managing director, Harry Broadhurst, spoke publicly about the close degree of cooperation between Rolls-Royce and Hawker Siddeley in developing the nacelle, pod and pylon to aerodynamically fit the Hatfield designed aft-loaded wing for the A.300 Airbus.

Donald Dykins, deputy chief aerodynamicist, Hawker Siddeley Aviation, also acknowledged the close degree of co-operation on the design of the A.300 that reached back on the European Airbus at least to July 1967. Dykins: 'Wind tunnel programme: The development for these models stretched from July 1967 to February of 1969. ... a lot of the development testing was done on 1/80th scale half-models in the Hatfield tunnel...'

Dykins also acknowledged that the majority of testing was carried out in house at Hatfield, where the wing and its under-wing engine pods were defined and handling and performances standards predicted.

Interestingly *Flight*, in September 1968, indicated that aero-dynamic research in Europe was travelling the same path that had been trodden by the Americans. Since the A.300 project development stemmed from the earlier HBN.100, the Europeans had been on similar paths since 1966 onwards. But whereas the Americans were focusing on a high bypass turbofan with short cowling for a second generation wing design, the Europeans were developing an engine power-plant influenced by a very advanced third generation wing design. For the European Airbus, the wing and the engine from 1967 onwards were, respectively, the responsibilities of Hawker Siddeley and Rolls-Royce.

> Anglo-French aerodynamic research for the A-300, though following some way behind similar paths travelled by the Americans with their C-5A and 747 ... There is evidence that British aero-dynamicists and mechanical engineers are working more closely together

than on the last generation of jet airliners. The A-300 is being specified ... with the power of two RB.207s ...

Flight emphasized the very close co-operation of engine and airframe designers and engineers in Europe. The fundamental difference between the European position and that of the Americans, who were constrained by the Curtiss-Wright patent agreement, must have been a considerable concern for the US companies and in particular for Lockheed and General Electric. Lockheed, as it experienced severe problems with the C5A's engines, tried several times to re-negotiate the contract to get GE to assume responsibility, but GE refused point blank.

The Rolls-Royce bids to supply the total power-plant packages for the DC-10, L1011 and A.300 airframes were separated by design nuances. As Blunt and Lupton point out, there were several designs of engine nacelles and mountings considered for the respective airframes: the DC-10 with central compressor mounting, the L1011 with a fan case mounting and the A.300 with core compressor pickup. The fact that the development engine was built with the core compressor mounting is significant evidence that Rolls-Royce was working very closely with Airbus and McDonnell-Douglas and geared up to supply engines to the A.300 and the DC-10.

Total Power-Plant Design

The scientific theory behind the use of the long nacelle in an integrated powerplant assumed a strategic importance for Rolls-Royce when it applied the innovative nacelle technologies in the commercial aero-engine business. These technologies provided the Rolls-Royce ATE bypass engines with a significant operating advantage over the competitors' products.

Roll-Royce understood that its control of the design of a fully integrated engine, intake, nacelle and pod in association with its pylon and wing is a primary function. The development and supply of a total power-plant package was the critical element that allowed the company to provide installed engine performance guarantees for its airline customers.

Newhouse, in 1982 wrote: 'The nacelle, or pod, houses the engine. It is among the most difficult parts of an airplane to design; the harmony that must be created between nacelle, engine and wing poses intricate structural and aerodynamic problems.'

Interestingly, it appears that Rolls-Royce were backing a two-way horse. In 1967, Wilde and Pickerell suggested that for all engine configurations, but with the proviso of certain exceptions, which would be influenced by wing design, a short cowling was the best solution. However, as would become quite clear with the unveiling, in 1968, of the Airbus A.300's advanced aft loaded wing, the joint Hawker Siddeley/Rolls-Royce nacelle, influenced by the revolutionary wing design, would be one of an intermediate and ¾ length, with inherent advantages in its design that outweighed the advantages usually associated with the short cowl.

A reflection of Rolls-Royce Hucknall's experience is shown in a page from a brochure for the Trent from 1967. (Rolls-Royce)

A Rolls-Royce model of an intermediate length nacelle power-plant used for testing. Apparent in this rear view of the power-plant and looking inside the nacelle is the aero-dynamic gear. (Author)

A Rolls-Royce model of an intermediate length nacelle power-plant used for testing. (Author)

Visible Support

Although the US Fairchild F-228 was the first aircraft to be launched with a fully integrated HBR pod designed by Rolls-Royce for the RB.203 Trent, one of the first airbus designs to benefit from the Rolls-Royce total propulsion package was the McDonnell-Douglas DC-10. The DC-10, as ordered by American Airlines, was to be powered with RB.211 engines, two of which would have been mounted underwing in Rolls-Royce signature intermediate length nacelles.

In early March 1968, McDonnell-Douglas issued an artist's impression of the DC-10 that had been ordered by American Airlines. In mid-March 1968, the American Airlines DC-10 was shown sporting the Rolls-Royce RB.211 engine power-plant design. The under wing position of the engine in an intermediate length nacelle with the long nacelle spine extending to almost the front of the nacelle are indicative of a similar Rolls-Royce RB.211 design used on the Lockheed L1011.

The picture was published in *Flight* on 7 March 1968 and its timing indicates that a decision to change the engine had yet to be taken. The publication of the picture was prior to C. R. Smith's approval by Congress as US Secretary of State for Commerce, a decision that was expected to take place in mid-March 1968.

Photo of a model of the Airbus A.300 with Rolls-Royce ATE RB.207 nacelle in BEA livery. (RAeS)

Airbus A.300 advert with RB.207 in an intermediate length engine nacelle designed in alignment with the HS Hatfield third generation aft-loaded wing.

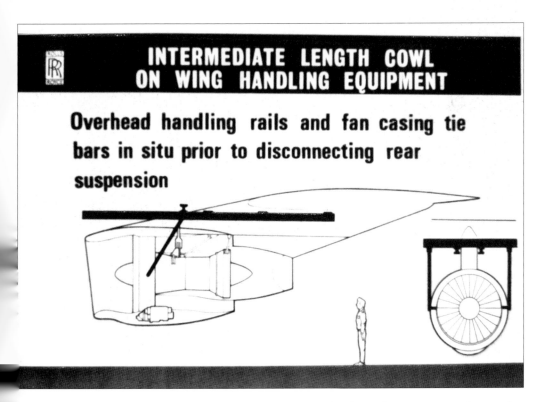

Intermediate length cowl on wing. A feature of the RB.207 for the Airbus A.300 was the on-wing handling equipment. (Rolls-Royce)

CHAPTER FOURTEEN

RESISTANCE AND DOMESTIC PARTIALITY

The US Moves to Block Rolls-Royce's Bid

On 7 March 1968, the Washington correspondent of *The Times* wrote:

> An attempt is being made in Congress to block Rolls-Royce's bid to supply engines for
> the projected United States airbus. Representative Robert Taft has marshalled opposition
> because of a report that Rolls-Royce has won approval for the engine.

The approval of the RB.211 by both the US president and US Treasury was substantiated
when on 9 March *The Times* reported that the Rolls-Royce bid had broken out into a
political row: President Johnson had received written protests from six Senators and five
Representatives, from Ohio and New Mexico – states that would benefit if a US maker
was selected. Their complaint was that 'not adequately balanced' information was given
during talks between representatives of airlines and the British government concerning the
American government's position on buying foreign engines.

American Airlines wanted to launch the McDonnell-Douglas DC-10 but it did not want
the General Electric engine. It seems that Kolk was free to choose the airframe, but not the
engines. In this case it seems most probable that the US administration was, again, running
a Buy American Policy.

Perhaps needled by the threat of the apparent 'success' of the British RB.211, the
US aero-engine industry engaged in a vigorous and ultimately successful rear-guard
action for 'domestic partiality'. The Military Industrial Complex made sure its position
was represented as it exerted its enormous pressure by vociferously lobbying the US
government. Senator Frank J. Lausch and Senator Robert Taft junior took up positions
of support for the US aviation industry where Trippe had just three years before. The
senators expressed their support for GE's position in particular as the US company with
the most to lose. They generated fear among their audiences as they spelled out the
consequences for the US aero-engine industry if US interests were ignored and an un-
American aero-engine purchase was made. (Gray 1971) They focused on what they felt
would be the drastic social and economic dislocations of American resources with wild
estimates of US job losses and US financial losses which must surely follow, if the US
government allowed US airlines to procure foreign Rolls-Royce engines. The sentiments

of US protectionism, or domestic partiality were rising in support of a Buy American Policy.

Representative of the scaremongering tactics used at the time and reported in *The Times*, the United States Congressman Robert Taft 'called for a congressional debate, [with] estimates that the projected market for the airbus would result in a United States payments deficit of $3,800 m. and a loss of 18,000 to 20,000 jobs'.

Underwing to Underhand

During 1966–67, the McDonnell aircraft company succeeded in merging with the Douglas Aircraft Company. The merger was achieved seamlessly, both politically and legally. On 27 April 1967, *Flight* reported that the shareholders of McDonnell and Douglas companies had voted overwhelmingly on 19 April to approve the merger. In a similar time frame, noises were being made which indicated a change of heart within the new Douglas company for different kind of aircraft than that outlined by Kolk.

Sensor, in the same issue of *Flight*, noted that American Airlines 'now seem less dogmatic about a twin'. Interestingly, under another separate article, *Flight* noted that the McDonnell and Douglas merger still had to be approved by the US Justice Department. Indicating the immense complexity that is the aviation industry, McDonnell was able to secure the Douglas company because it had been granted financial assistance that was approved by the US administration. These points may indicate that the US administration had been persuaded by the UK Labour government of the benefits of adopting a medium-size advanced Rolls-Royce engine and an early strategy may have been formulated between the UK and the US to deliver up Rolls-Royce to US interests.

Politics All the Way

It appears that the political considerations of the US administration were in the vanguard, ready to protect the US Department of Defense's high by-pass technology and repel the threat of the American 'Jumbo Twin' and its foreign economics which were driven by the Rolls-Royce ATE RB.207. In contrast to the repositioning of the US industry that was sought by McNamara, the US administration was to step in again in support of US interests against the threat of foreign technology.

In what appeared to have been a US political move designed to stymie the threat posed to US interests by the high probability of a sole power-plant supply in favour of the British Rolls-Royce RB.211 on the McDonnell-Douglas DC-10, the White House stepped into the fray and leant its support to the US protectionist lobby. The White House did need the US military industrial complex after all.

Pugh addresses this issue in his account of the history of Rolls-Royce:

American Airlines was to announce in March 1968 an order for the DC-10 to be powered by RB211. U.S president Lyndon Johnson announced the appointment of President of American [Airlines] Cyrus R. Smith as Secretary of State for Commerce. Under the circumstances, American felt it would be embarrassing to announce it had chosen an aero engine for its new aircraft made by a foreign company.

Despite months of competitive commercial wrangling between the aircraft and engine makers that eventually decided in favour of the DC-10 and RB.211 combination it seems that a decision more favourably directed towards overall US interests was required. A decision that would counter the perceived position of British technical superiority, and protect US prestige, and to this effect, McDonnell-Douglas succumbed to US administrative pressure and pursued the General Electric engine. David Boulton wrote: '[McDonnell] Douglas had bowed to Congressional grumblings at the industry's lack of patriotism and left their more robust rivals to link up with the foreigner.'

The arguments put forward by US institutions and organizations in favour of US aviation companies were vote-sensitive social and political issues. Commercial and technical factors, it seemed, were not as important. The US administration promoted the principles of free trade in commercial considerations and overall only such principles should influence the selection of an engine for the US plane. However, as Galbraith notes:

> Only someone with an instinct for inconvenience suggests that firms such as Lockheed or General Dynamics, which do most of their business with the government, make extensive use of plants owned by government, have their working capital supplied by the government, have their cost overruns socialised by government ... are anything but the purest manifestations of private enterprise. (Galbraith, 1973)

For anyone to consider or believe that the politically and strategically important US aviation industry could survive in a politically unsupported, commercial world free from any US government protection is asking too much. Without the political clout generated by the US aviation's noisy clamour for attention, the British Rolls-Royce company would have secured the engine orders. As it stands, Douglas bowed to Congressional pressure and the RB.211's technology was directly purchased by Lockheed and Britain was forced to collaborate on terms dictated by Washington.

As Hayward argued, the 'ameliorative' effect of direct purchase is a form of co-operation and collaboration. But the true 'test of collaboration comes when one national perception comes into conflict with others. In addition', Hayward wrote, 'there are always ways in which a national government can stall, pressure or otherwise compromise collaborative arrangements, and ultimately the project itself. Collaborative projects are from inception to production opportunities for political choice...'

Buried in the Tail

As the respected industry journal *Engineering* noted in a before and after story of the RB.211's US success, commercial considerations were placed second to vote sensitive political factors:

> Politics all the way – this has been the story of the Rolls-Royce RB211 three shaft turbofan engine ... international politics have little favoured the three-shaft family ... American

balance of payments trouble, Congressional opposition, have both been against the RB.211.

The article in *Engineering* provides visual references of the advanced state of ATE progress. A photograph shows a mock up of the fan duct, its aperture centred on engineers working on the first development RB.211-06. The photograph clearly shows the engine with a compressor case-mounted accessory gearbox. Located in the same article and above the photograph is a cutaway impression of an RB211 engine displaying an accessory gearbox mounted in the nacelle.

Perhaps with more than a hint of suspicion of what the outcome would be, the article in *Engineering* concluded by asking: 'Which engine will McDonnell Douglas fit in the DC-10 airbuses for American Airlines?'

Rolls-Royce's over-reach was gradually nearing its disastrous consequence.

CHAPTER FIFTEEN

CLOSING THE TECHNOLOGY GAP

The US aero-engine manufacturers were of course lobbying for their own engines to power the US McDonnell Douglas DC-10. GE was offering the CF6, an engine that had been derived from the US government-funded military TF39. The alternative Pratt & Whitney engine, although having been ruled out of the competition by the airlines, was still a compatriot resisting the British invasion.

The commercial CF6 aero-engine from GE was based on the same engine core as was developed for the TF39. The TF39 engine had an overall length, from fan to nozzle plug flange, of 204 inches or 5,180 mm. In its dressed form the TF39 1C is 312 inches or 7,900 mm long. The CF6-6 appears slightly shorter than the TF39, with a bare engine length of 188 inches or 4,780 mm.

GE's TF-39 engine was a worry for everybody, including the US Department of Defense, which had funded the acquisition of the strategic technologies. As such, GE's commercial aero-engine position was a very good indicator of the limits of their industrial capability, the limits of their technical knowledge, their commercial disadvantage, and of the likelihood of their engine's inability to generate US Treasury revenues for their political sponsor, the US DoD.

General Electric, by Brian Rowe's own admission, was not able to address the technical issues of the CF6 which, awkwardly, imposed economic and safety issues on the DC-10:

> Frank Kolk of American [Airlines] was one of the people concerned with the length of our engine. Because everybody seemed to be worried about it, we offered to warranty the problem. We also suggested to Kolk that he put flags on the tails of the airplanes to warn everybody. He did not appreciate the suggestion.

GE had to do something about its engine to engage with Kolk, yet it could not shorten its engine to the extent required and neither did GE have the experience nor the resources in house to supply McDonnell-Douglas with a complete and integrated HBR power-plant package. If GE were not able to match the foreign engine's technical merits, it could make life unbearable for Rolls-Royce by raising the political heat through its extensive connections in the Senate and the House of Representatives.

GE Fights Back

GE, in its bid to persuade US politicians of the economic unfairness of the proposed British engine trade in the US, questioned the level of UK government subsidy claimed by Rolls-Royce for the RB.211. GE claimed that UK government financial support allowed Rolls-Royce to offer US airlines a very low engine price, albeit some would argue, for a paper engine. In early 1968 *The Times* reported: 'As to price competition, General Electric claimed that its price reflected development costs financed by the company, whereas the Rolls-Royce price reflected development costs subsidized by the British Government.'

General Electric has never denied that the US taxpayers funded, through the USAF/US government Department of Defense, its high by-pass ratio technology acquisition programme. The GE TF-39 high by-pass ratio turbofan aero-engine and its development were paid for entirely with US government help. General Electric received nearly $20 million in DoD funding during 1964/65 to cover design and development of the GE-1 scaled prototype, in addition to being awarded $458 million for the initial TF39 contract. The total cost of the GE TF39 engine development has been estimated to have reached over $1 billion.

Prior to the massive financial award for the development of the USAF TF39, General Electric had never built a twin-spool engine for service and the new technology HBR TF39 was going to be its first twin-spool aero-engine design for operational use. Rolls-Royce on the other hand had been designing and testing twin-spool engines since the RB.39 Clyde, which first ran in August 1945, and also benefited from BED's experience with the BS.75, the BS.100, the Olympus and the Pegasus engines. GE's first full-size block one engine ran on its test bed in January 1966. A GE history suggests that the block one engine was brought to test in December 1965.

Knaack noted that GE's entry into the twin-spool and high bypass ratio turbofan technology was not easy:

As should have been expected, the early testing revealed various technical problems. In January 1966, the first full-scale engine, after just three hours of accumulated testing time, failed because of a faulty bearing retainer. When testing resumed, the re-built engine lost three first-stage turbine blades when fatigue cracking appeared at stress concentration points.

The TF39's installed performance and airframe integration issues continued on beyond the flight test programme with the associated increases in costs, which were in addition to the total price procurement contract, funded by the USAF. The acquisition of the HBR technology in the development of the TF39 caused GE to overspend in relation to its total procurement price contract and this was reflected in the almost continuous engine upgrades. GE was unable to provide the USAF with an engine capable of producing the original brochure performance until late in the TF39's program life.

Bare Essentials

GE's position as a US producer and supplier of bare engines was typical. During the period up until 1975, when the aircraft patent pool agreement was in force, the aircraft designer

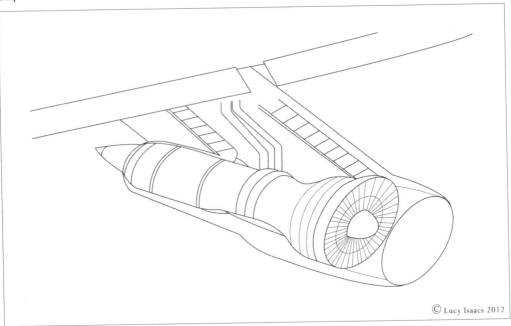

© Lucy Isaacs 2012

A close up of the TF39 engine for the C5A. The two ladder type attachments between the engine and the wing indicate the positions of the engine mountings. (Lucy Isaacs)

A General Electric TF39 on a Lockheed C5A. This picture clearly displays the short nacelle and the parallel cold air fan cowl and is indicative of a lack of the aerodynamic gear.

and development engineers were responsible for the aero-dynamic performance of the engine pod and the effects of nacelle drag and interference on the wing.

For the Lockheed C-5A, the TF39 pylon and cowl were designed by Lockheed and built by Rohr Industries. Rohr were at the time the world's largest supplier of engine cowls and nacelles, having supplied the engine pods for the P&W engines on the 707 and DC-8. Unfortunately for Lockheed, the problems associated with the TF39 engine integration on the C5A were Lockheed's alone as it was the design authority for the nacelle, pod, and pylon and contractually ultimately responsible too for the integrated engine's installed performance. As engine problems escalated, neither the USAF nor GE nor Rohr would heed Lockheed's requests to renegotiate the contract and take responsibility for the engine's installation and related performance issues.

Completion of the B-52E/TF39 testing program did not mean that all engine tests were over or that every engine problem was solved. The problems that remained did not seem especially serious, however. For example, in October 1969 the TF39 aft engine mount, located on the turbine's mid-frame, failed during a static test, but the failure did not affect on-going flight tests or the normal operation of the C–5As being delivered to the Military Airlift Command (MAC), as MATS had been redesignated in January 1966. (Knaack 1998)

A CF6 turbofan nacelle. The intermediate length nacelle together with the flared turbine casing are an indication of the influence of Rolls-Royce and the use of Dawson's aerodynamic gear.

With the installation performance responsibility issues surrounding the military TF39 engine, which were still unresolved by the time the civil CF6 was being suggested for use on commercial aircraft, it is no stretch of the imagination to understand that in the commercial aviation world the proposed General Electric CF6 was a very high risk engine in relation to the RB.211.

In Kolk's considered opinion the bare GE engine was, at over five metres, too long; Boeing thought the GE engine was a smoker; it was generally acknowledged that the GE engine was very noisy; and GE had been absent from the commercial transport market for almost ten years.

In their bid to get the CF6 onto the DC-10, GE and Rohr had a significant dilemma on their hands. Could McDonnell-Douglas have completed the necessary design changes to the aircraft, in support of the DC-10's in-service performance guarantees for the airlines, especially within the time frame it had allowed itself? Could the power-plant design changes that would have been necessitated by a late change in engine selection, changes for instance to the pod/pylon and wing design, so as to minimise airflow interference, have been completed to the degree to allow the airlines to be confident in pursuing the GE re-engined DC10 as a commercially viable project?

If the DC-10 was going to be supplied with GE engines then the airlines wanted reassurances from GE and Rohr that they were technically capable of dealing with the airlines' concerns to the degree that had already been proposed by Rolls-Royce.

Chula Vista

In the case of the RB.211, Rolls-Royce was prepared to give installed power-plant performance assurances. General Electric would have had to at least match Rolls-Royce's assurances to be able to begin to convince both McDonnell Douglas and American Airlines that they could do the job. Brian Rowe acknowledged the difficulty there would be in trying to persuade the airlines to accept the CF6 in place of the British engine in light of the UK company's advantage:

> Rolls-Royce had promised McDonnell-Douglas an integrated engine-nacelle package. The nacelle, that streamlined enclosure for the engine, can be a complex highly specialised piece of work. We really had not wanted to get involved in that part of the aerodynamic design, but we had to get McDonnell-Douglas to accept our engine. Ted Stigwolt, Ron Welch, and I got on a plane and went to Rohr Industries to convince them to design and build the nacelle. McDonnell-Douglas would have a strong say in the design, but GE would be the system manager for the integrated nacelle. Getting Rohr to agree was relatively easy, but the people at McDonnell-Douglas seemed to be dragging their feet, with no-one willing to accept responsibility to approve the package.
>
> After hashing out details until 10.30 one evening, I spent the rest of the night writing an agreement. In it, I described how we would work together, how we would make the integrated nacelle system work, how we would make it so that the engines could be overhauled on the wing, and then I signed it for GE. In the morning I gave the agreement to McDonnell-Douglas representatives and said, 'GE will stand behind this.' This was subsequently known as the Chula Vista agreement and was one of the first working

together programmes in the industry. It ended up enabling us to build a much better nacelle and a more maintainable engine. (Rowe 2005)

It was a significant event in the history of aviation and of the development of the high by-pass ratio turbofan aero-engine when General Electric changed its supply stance to include the provision of a complete integrated engine-nacelle package for the CF6, in effect mirroring Rolls-Royce's design and supply positions. Yet how did the companies involved get hold of the technologies to enable them to mirror Rolls-Royce's position in the short time frame?

General Electric's Credit

GE, to its credit, had developed and supplied the USAF with the innovative TF39 high by-pass ratio large turbofan engine for the very large Lockheed C-5A military transport. GE's assumption, and McNamara's view, was that the unduplicated technology that GE had developed would transfer straight over into the commercial market as the CTF-39. However, both Boeing and Pan American refused to take the engine for the 747, as it was a military engine that was unsuitable for commercial service, being too noisy, too smoky, and too long and engineered for a relatively slow speed.

GE, in late 1967, realised that it would have to redesign its TF39 to make it commercially attractive to US airlines. The outcome of that decision was the launch in October 1967 of the CF6 engine, the commercial version of the TF39, an engine that was almost totally paid for by the US taxpayer. The CF6, by comparison, was designed with a by-pass ratio of 6:1, together with features which produced less noise and was therefore a more fitting aero-engine proposition for the commercial DC-10.

In addressing the commercialization of GE's high by-pass TF39 turbofan, Brian Rowe acknowledged a shortcoming in the engine's twin-spool technology. He admitted that the TF39 needed improving, and in particular the 'compressor rotor really did need a redesign. The rotor we proposed – actually, the way the rotor was held together - would be heavier, but it would last much longer and be more easily maintained'. (Rowe 2005)

This allowed GE to shorten the CF6 shaft by 20 inches over the TF39 so that it might reduce the whirling issues associated with the military engine. Paolo Lironi notes that the

earlier [CF6] models received criticism for being long giving the engine a tendency for the shafts to bend in use. The consequence of this excessive bending was significant rubbing of blade tips resulting in a high rate of engine performance deterioration and higher removal and overhaul rates. (Lironi 2007)

In addition, a major problem known to the commercial airlines was that GE provided only the bare engines to the USAF and distanced itself from any of the problems which Lockheed and the USAF experienced with engine integration and related performance shortfalls on the C-5A aircraft.

However, and significantly, GE had learned a hard lesson and was not going to repeat the mistake that it had committed on the C-5A by not providing an integrated engine solution.

This time, with its CF6 for the commercial market, GE would focus on an integrated power-plant for the DC-10 that was to be designed by McDonnell Douglas, built by Rohr and managed by GE. Accordingly, the respective costs associated with designing and building the integrated power-plant for the DC-10 would not be borne by GE, whereas for the RB.211 the total development costs and therefore the price of the Rolls-Royce RB.211 engine included the design and testing of the complete power-plant. Thus emphasizing to an even greater degree the higher value for money package Rolls-Royce were able to provide on the DC-10 in relation to its US competitor.

The battle between the US industry, aided by its patriotic supporters and vested interest groups, and the sole UK power-plant supplier assumes, in a manner, an ideological argument, one where the lines are drawn between revolution or continuity, and between autonomous or joint responsibility. It was almost like witnessing the American Revolution all over again but with the US assuming the dictatorial role of the autocrat. As Zeigler pointed out, an airline chose an engine because it preferred Gothic or Roman architecture.

This period in aviation history effectively marks the end of the Total Procurement Package contract era, although variations of the style still continued. Referring back to costs and total responsibility, the companies involved GE, Rohr and McDonnell Douglas all assumed the responsibilities for their specialisms. Their joint co-operation and responsibility mirrored the input of each of the creative forces employed by Rolls-Royce and Hawker Siddeley, together with Airbus for the design of the A.300. As Rowe noted, the separate US companies working together had produced a better nacelle/pod that was in stark contrast to the performance of Lockheed's sole design and production effort on the C-5A/TF39 nacelle and pod.

Rowe's conclusion is supported when one considers that the Boeing-designed cowl and pod, which were built by Rohr to Boeing's command to house the P&W JT9D engine on the 747, suffered the disastrous effects of ovalisation.

A Foregone Conclusion

Robert McNamara left the US Department of Defense on 29 February 1968 to take up the presidency of the World Bank.

The engine decision for the DC-10 dragged on until finally, towards the end of April 1968, the parties involved agreed and United Airlines placed an order for thirty DC-10s and thirty options and specified the US General Electric CF6 as the aero-engine. Despite leaving its competitors at the starting gate, American Airlines followed United's decision and ordered the GE engine.

GE was not only going to supply the very latest high by-pass ratio aero-engine technology on a new airframe with an engine that, in Kolk's view, was second best but crucially it was going to enter into the supply of engines for the commercial aircraft market on a scale and cost where it would have to match the worldwide presence of its established and experienced competitors. As Boyne suggests, American would never have ordered the Lockheed aircraft because of credibility issues and to an extent similar issues were voiced at GE by airlines. GE's commercial credibility was virtually non-existent and as Brian Rowe admitted, GE had an uphill struggle to overcome:

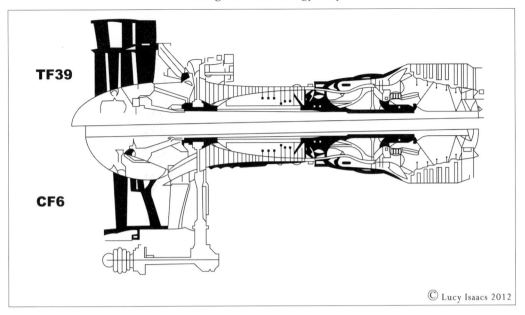

The structural differences between the General Electric TF39 and CF6. (Lucy Isaacs)

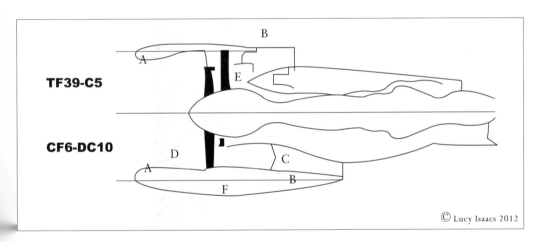

Emphasising the differences between the nacelle of the CF6 and the TF39, this illustration highlights the CF6's longer cowl, the thicker intake lip and the use of Rolls-Royce's aero-dynamic gear. A: Lip, increased thickness on engine inlet ring; B: Nacelle length, increased to intermediate length; C: Aerodynamic gear; D: Single large fan; E: Inlet and outlet guide vanes reduced; F: Gearbox and accessories in nacelle. These differences are the key to the changes made to the TF39 and made the CF6 more representative of the Rolls-Royce RB.211. (Lucy Isaacs)

Although we had a long history with military customers, our commercial experience was incredibly thin. (Rowe 2005)

However, in regards to these points it was GE that had developed the world's first high by-pass ratio turbofan for the US Air Force so that the new and very large carrier aircraft could deliver the 'US' anywhere in the world. Anywhere in the world would also translate for GE into a US Air Force requirement for spare engines and engine parts to be positioned anywhere in the world, effectively providing GE with a US government-funded engineering network to support its new commercial business. However, this advantage would be provided at a reduced commercial cost, thereby providing further evidence of US subsidies in support of American free trade principles.

As Charles Stuart pointed out, there were strategic and military benefits which overlapped civil aviation's use of the new wide-body technologies. In addition, significant monies would be required on a grand and international scale, so much so that the trade would influence the economics of countries.

The rarely talked about geo-political connections and their influence on the civil air transport, and that industry's economics, which Stuart addressed were not lost on the US industry and its supporters. The UK would be dependent on a duplicitous US.

CHAPTER SIXTEEN

ROLLS-ROYCE SHORT CIRCUITED

Rolls-Royce, with its complete power-plant strategy, fully integrated itself with the aircraft programmes. The British engineers firmly embedded themselves in all aspects of the power-plant, from its design through to contractually guaranteeing the installed performance of the total power-plant propulsion system.

Rolls-Royce's innovative customer-focused approach was a wake-up call to the American aviation industry in many ways. Most importantly, it challenged the power of the airframe designer over the critically important issue of installed power-plant performance. Equally as important, it placed the responsibility for total engine power-plant design and integration with the engine manufacturer. Just as important, the strategy devised by Rolls-Royce established the direct communication between operators and the manufacturer for all aspects relating to the power-plant, thus by-passing the political intrigues that sometimes influenced aircraft manufacturers.

The information released by Rolls-Royce at the Paris Airshow in June 1967 clearly indicated the company's direction and intentions towards the development of the new turbofan technologies which would be employed on its family of high by-pass ratio turbofans. *Flight International* featured a cutaway drawing of the three-shaft HBR Rolls-Royce ATE RB.207 'selected for the final pre-go-ahead design studies on the Anglo-French-German airbus'.

Supporting Rolls-Royce's commitment towards the development of its high by-pass ratio ATE turbofan family, the company displayed a complete pod for the RB.203 Trent installation at Paris. The RB.203 nacelle shown at Paris was a clear visual representation of Dawson's theory; its subtle lines heralded significant change for the aviation industry.

The appearance of the ATE RB.203 pod at Paris in June 1967 is important for several reasons. Firstly, it indicated the positioning of the gearbox accessories off the engine core. Secondly, the location of the gearbox accessories influenced the design and shape of the RB.203 nacelle. One can see in the accompanying picture the deeper profile of the underside of the nacelle. Thirdly, the nacelle's intermediate length extends along the engine exiting at the position of the turbine. 'Although the Trent is relatively small, Rolls-Royce feels the principle is applicable to engines up to 50,000 lbs of thrust.' (*Science News* 1967)

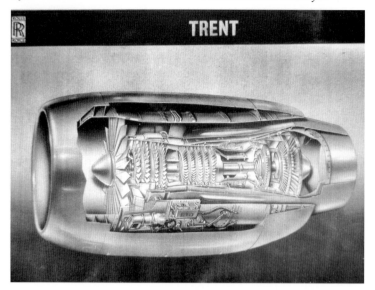

An early cutaway diagram of the three-shaft Rolls-Royce Trent and representative of the RB.207. The diagram clearly indicates the location of the gearbox accessories within the nacelle of the high by-pass turbofan. The pod was constructed by Short Brothers. (Rolls-Royce)

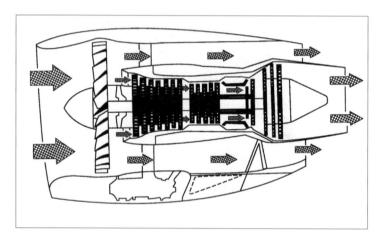

This general arrangement diagram of the RB.211 shows air flow through an intermediate length nacelle on a three-shaft engine. (Author)

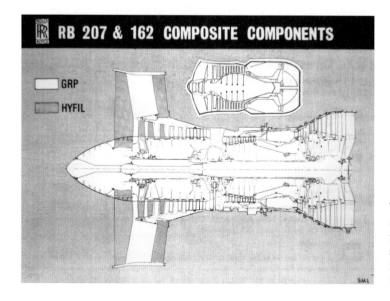

The RB.207, like the 203 and 211, was designed to use hyfil in the engine structure, OGVs and the intermediate compressor. (Rolls-Royce)

RB.207 Leading particulars

(Contract Specification gives all relevant weight and performance
adjustments and guarantee points to suit current Request
for Proposal of the constructor)

Max. take-off thrust . . . . . . 47,500 lb.(up to 90°F)
Growth is programmed

Weight . . . . 8,584 lb.(Max. basic dry)
Thrust/weight 5.55

Max. cruise rating
(35,000 ft., 0.85 Mach No. I.S.A.)
Net Thrust . . . . 10,280 lb
Specific fuel consumption . . . . . 0.62 lb./hr/lb.(Max)

Dimensions
Intake diameter . . . . 100.94 in.
Length . . . . 125.85ins.(Intake face to
exhaust flange)

Note: Performance values do not include installation losses

The leading particulars for the RB.207. This was going to be the engine for the A.300.
(Rolls-Royce)

The US Adapts

In early 1967, *Flight* further described the ATE RB.203 Trent:

> The Rolls-Royce Trent is a third generation turbofan of three shaft layout and advanced
> in terms of materials and compactness. With an initial take off thrust rating of 9,730lb the
> RB.203-01 is said to embody considerable thrust growth potential.. The Trent is aimed
> specifically at the requirements of the short haul operator in the 1970s ... So far the Trent
> is a private venture program ... The first Trent is expected to run at the end of this year and
> the first pair of flight engines will be delivered to Fairchild Hiller in the summer of 1968.

Lockheed attributed the technical authority of one of the key features of the intermediate
nacelle to Rolls-Royce: 'An innovation that was first introduced by Rolls-Royce was the
mounting of the engine accessories external to the fan exhaust duct where they are driven
by a shaft extension.' (Frisbee 1974)

Frisbee's acknowledgement of Rolls-Royce Limited as the author and owner of the
intellectual property and as the designer of the intermediate length high by-pass ratio
power-plant nacelle is supported by Blunt and Lupton. As their early 1968 paper clearly
indicates, Rolls-Royce were aware of power-plant nacelle drag, integration and wing
interference issues for a considerable time prior to their paper's publication. The issues of
mechanical complexity, aerodynamics and materials were logically extended and addressed
in Dawson's pod theory. In a paper delivered by Sir Stanley Hooker for the Fifty-Eighth
Wilbur and Orville Wright Memorial Lecture at the Royal Aeronautical Society in December
1969, Hooker described the three factors which attributed to the dramatic development of
he gas turbine from the Avon to the (ATE) RB.211:

The skill of the designer in overcoming the mechanical complexities of concentric shafts driving independent compressors in series.

Aerodynamic research which allows compressor blade tip speeds to be supersonic without appreciable loss in efficiency.

Material developments which allow higher turbine operating temperatures, particularly in combination with air-cooled blades.

The creative skill of the designer, along with aerodynamic research and material development were all key elements which attributed to the superior performance of the RB.203. The design and research for the Trent was started back in 1964 while development work on the Rolls-Royce ATE RB.203 Trent triple-spool high by-pass turbofan was started in July 1966, and later the same year its details were revealed to the public at SBAC Farnborough. Fifteen months later, in December 1967, the revolutionary engine that was privately funded by Rolls-Royce was proving its technologies and delivering its expected performance. A Rolls-Royce main board member giving evidence to the DTi report authors spoke of the company's confidence of developing the private venture Trent:

> We then introduced, or started to introduce, an engine called the Trent, which was never fully developed but it was developed to the stage where we were getting very satisfactory performances from it. Its importance was that it was the first three-shaft engine.

GE CF6 nacelle access, from a 1969 brochure. (GE brochure AEG 5/69-138E via RAeS)

The RB.203 took Rolls-Royce into the higher realms of aero-engine technologies and engine performances, which were beyond the second generation high by-pass technology available to GE and P&W.

Short Changed

In March 1967, the chairman of Shorts, Mr Cuthbert Wrangham was told by the Ministry of Technology that he was required to 'leave Shorts' at the end of the year; 'Others knew of his dismissal even earlier. The reason for it has never been made plain and that has been enough to make several otherwise eligible candidates fight clear ...'

Rolls-Royce, in 1967 had contracted Short Brothers & Harland in Northern Ireland, a company that at the time was majority owned by the UK government and under the remit of Mintech, to build its nacelle for the RB.203. A RB.203 nacelle was ready for display at Paris in June 1967.

It is most probable that Rolls-Royce froze the design and initiated production work for the building of the RB.211-06 development engines in June 1967, some 15 months in advance of the first test run of the 06 series in August 1968. In early 1968, Rolls-Royce also contracted Shorts to build the nacelle for the RB.211.

In late 1967 and early 1968, the UK government Ministry of Technology held talks with the US Rohr corporation with a view to trading Shorts. There were several meetings between the two sides as they tried to bridge the gap in negotiations but to no avail and the talks collapsed in late 1968. After Rolls-Royce had secured the L1011 engine contract, a spokesman for Rolls-Royce reiterated its position on the supply of the RB.211 power-plant for the L1011:

> Rolls-Royce is to supply the complete powerplant pack to Lockheed. It will include intake, reverser, silencer nozzle, pod and pylon. The intake, pods and pylons have been subcontracted to Shorts, for whom this will be most valuable long term business.... The entire powerplant is to be built in Britain and there is no question of subcontract work to American companies.

This supply position, I suggest, was a reflection of a similar agreement that Rolls-Royce would have had on the DC-10.

All Change is no Change

McDonnell-Douglas had stipulated that additional orders would be needed to secure the DC-10 programme, and that it would limit the time available to receive the anticipated orders to a maximum of three months from the time of American's order. In addition, Rolls-Royce had also set a time limit of the end of April 1968 for the proposed supply of its RB.211 for the DC-10.

As Rolls-Royce would have been the design authority for the entire DC-10 power-plant, as a consequence of the early retirement of the RB.211 from the DC-10 engine competition McDonnell-Douglas would have had no other supplier that could have replaced the Rolls-

Royce designed integrated power-plant with an engine package that offered exactly the same performance.

This would have presented significant and expensive engineering problems to both GE and McDonnell-Douglas, which they would have had to address in a very limited time frame.

The influences, for instance, of the aero-dynamic interferences from a specific CF6 nacelle, pod and pylon would interact differently on the DC-10's wing from those of the RB.211 power-plant design. A complete redesign of the engine and wing integration from the start would be very expensive. The redesign efforts would also be severely limited by time constraints and the possible engineered solutions would probably be contrary to what American Airlines expected from its engine supplier.

The cheaper and quicker alternative to redesigning the wing, pylon and nacelle configuration and to minimizing the aero-dynamic effects of a design specifically geared to the CF6, would be to maintain the existing power-plant design and to fit the GE CF6 into the space that had been vacated by the proposed Rolls-Royce designed nacelle and pod.

I suggest that once it had been decided that McDonnell-Douglas and American were going to use the US CF6 high by-pass engine, the airframe and the airline customers would dictate how the engine would be integrated onto the DC-10. Literature produced by General Electric at about this time explained the consequent selection of GE's CF-6 engine for the DC-10 citing the influences of the (American) airline customers on design features of the engine. GE's acknowledgement of the airline customers' authority and influence indicates to me the engine maker's acceptance of the parameters into which they would have to fit.

Artist's impression of the DC-10 from an early GE brochure. (GE brochure AEG 5/69-138E via RAeS)

R-R is Left with a High Tech Engine Looking for an Airframe

Were McDonnell Douglas persuaded by outside influences to stall the engine choice so as to make time available to the other engine manufacturers, who would then lodge a renewed effort to secure the DC-10 engine business, possibly using similar airline contract specifications to those offered by Rolls-Royce? In 1970, *Flight* revisited Douglas:

> We asked whether Douglas would be prepared to install the RB.211. 'We would certainly listen. Rolls-Royce keep us posted and there is close liaison. We would ask what's the deal?' No. there was no gentleman's agreement by anybody with anybody not to fit the Rolls engine in the DC-10. Such an agreement by an engine manufacturer would, in Douglas's view, be impossible these days. They had great respect for Rolls-Royce. It was 'highly unlikely' that Douglas would finance any engineering or certification of the RB.211 in the DC-10.

McDonnell-Douglas seemed to regret not having the Rolls-Royce engine on the DC-10; however their strenuous denial of any agreement to keep the RB.211 off of the DC-10 rings hollow.

Was Rolls-Royce Limited asked to make way for General Electric's competing product to power the DC-10? It seems the answer was provided by Mintech via Shorts and Rohr.

I suggest that US vested interests tried to obtain, through Rohr, the Rolls-Royce high bypass duct technologies which appeared on the RB.203 nacelle and pod. As the nacelle technologies were scaleable, and with Shorts awarded the RB.211 nacelle contract in early 1968, I suggest Rohr increased its efforts to secure the technologies, and that these efforts took place in a similar time frame when the Chula Vista agreement was being forged. Such a scenario would go a long way to explaining how GE and Rohr suddenly found they had the resources to supply a similar high by-pass duct technology to that of Rolls-Royce for the CF6 on the DC-10.

CHAPTER SEVENTEEN

TECHNOLOGY CROSSOVER

By the time that C. R. Smith had been confirmed as the new US Secretary of State for Commerce, McDonnell-Douglas and American Airlines issued the definitive general-arrangement drawing of the DC-10 series 10.

There are a number of points I shall address regarding the general arrangement drawing of the DC-10, which were definitive of the aircraft ordered by American Airlines. The first is that the power-plant arrangement is similar to the artist's impression of the DC-10 issued by McDonnell-Douglas and reported by *Flight* on 7 March. The second point is that the under-wing engine nacelle seems to be identical to the 7 March picture representation. The third point is that this drawing was issued after the appointment of C. R. Smith as US Secretary of Commerce was confirmed, which suggests continuity of the earlier Rolls-Royce influenced design of the under-wing power-plant.

Had a decision on engine selection for American Airlines been taken by the time the definitive general arrangement drawing for the DC-10 was issued on 21 March 1968? Was the timing of the drawing's public issue related to the confirmation of C. R. Smith's appointment as US Secretary of Commerce? Was Smith's appointment conditional on American Airlines reversing its decision to order British Rolls-Royce engines and replace them with US General Electric engines? It is during this phase of the DC-10's evolution that I suggest that Brian Rowe put together the Chula Vista agreement.

Significantly, the definitive GA drawing of the American Airlines DC-10 indicates the continuing influence on the DC-10 of the intermediate length nacelle power-plant design. The continuing influence of the original Rolls-Royce design indicates that a technology crossover probably occurred between the dates attributed to the drawings. The GA drawing also indicates that, in the context of timing, the US was satisfied with the arrangement, witness Smith's confirmed appointment as US Secretary of Commerce.

By the end of April 1968, the RB.211 option on the DC-10 had expired and in early May McDonnell-Douglas announced it had awarded the engine contract to General Electric for its CF6. Provisional data on the CF6 powered DC-10 was provided in *Flight*:

Powerplant: Three 39,500lb-thrust GE CF6/36-6.

MCDONNELL DOUGLAS has published the first specification and performance details

An Iberia DC-10 Series 10 with CF6 intermediate length nacelles.

of the DC-10. So far 110 aircraft of the type have been ordered (American Airlines, 25 plus 25 option; and United Air Lines, 30 plus 30 on option).

Not since the days of Boeing 707 and Douglas DC-8 rivalry has there been a pair of such closely similar aircraft as the DC-10 and the Lockheed 1011. In all other respects the rival claims are virtually identical. The two-versus-three-spool rival engine philosophy is the only major point of overall design difference.

There appears to be no changes to the exterior design of the under wing nacelles, and the nacelles continue the intermediate length cowl design as proposed by Rolls-Royce for the original American DC-10 order. The continuity of the external nacelle features suggests that GE and Rohr had obtained the Rolls-Royce ATE high bypass duct technologies.

Space for Hypotheses

At this juncture, it is interesting to note the development changes that the TF-39 sported as GE tried to commercialize its military engine technology for use on the DC-10. The most important of these were described by *Flight* in an article that was published on 5 October 1967.

The *Flight* article lays out the specification of the GE CF6. The CF6 was based on the military TF39, and was the engine contender for the next generation wide-body DC-10 and L1011. It had a design thrust of 34,000 lbst, a by-pass ratio of 6, a weight of 6,975 lbs and an overall pressure ratio of 25.1. 'The front fan has been specially designed to minimise noise, there are no inlet guide vanes, large outlet vane clearances and integrated suppression materials in the cowl wall.'

Sometime after GE displayed a CF6 mock-up with the accessory drive mounted on the core, as in the picture above, the company again changed the engine layout.

In this later cutaway drawing of the CF-6, the revised engine layout features the gearbox located in the nacelle fan case, similar to that devised by Rolls-Royce on the RB.211 for the L1011. Similarly, GE's decision to relocate the accessory drive would have necessitated the adoption of an intermediate to long cowl.

Another interesting feature of the revised CF6 as identified by Bill Gunston, one of the world's foremost aviation writers, in his insightful work *The Development of Jet and Turbine Aero Engines* was the CF6 engine power-plant designer or development engineer's adopted use of the pod bulge. 'The amount of space between the core and the bulging inner cowl is unusual.' (Gunston 2007)

The bulge indicates the aerodynamic gear which reduces air velocity at the bypass exit, thus lowering the bypass air speed and increasing thrust. Thompson and Smith highlighted the operational attributes of the three quarter length cowl. Within their description are the design-influenced attributes which have been visibly adopted by GE for use on its CF6 aero-engine and therefore provide an explanation for the unusual bulging inner cowl: '...this duct length, together with the externally located accessories of the RB.211 engine, minimises the duct curvature and allows a low duct velocity to be selected.'

Thus, with the aerodynamic gear's appearance on the CF6, Dawson's scientifically formulated design for increasing the overall operating efficiency of an intermediate or long duct for an advanced Rolls-Royce high bypass aero-engine found its way onto a US engine at an opportune moment for GE in its battle to power the DC-10.

Significantly and clearly, the GE CF6 engine shared a number of features which also appeared on the Rolls-Royce RB.211 three-shaft high by-pass ratio aero-engine. The most important of these were the adoption of the aerodynamic gear, the intermediate length nacelle and the relocation of the gearbox accessory drive from the engine core to the fan case. The CF6 nacelle's air intake lip profile also differed from the original technology developed on the TF39, and as a result of a deeper profile the improved CF6 intake performance proved superior to that of the original TF39 air intake.

Rolls-Royce Limited were not in an unfamiliar situation. Having worked very closely with McDonnell-Douglas and American Airlines to develop the RB.211-06/10 for the McDonnell-Douglas DC-10, the prize order was removed from their grip. The apparent removal of the foreign RB.211 by US political interests placed Rolls-Royce Limited in a very vulnerable position.

Back in 1966, Boeing had asked Rolls-Royce to pitch their RB.178 high by-pass turbofan technology in competitive tender for use on the 747. That engine supply deal went to Pratt & Whitney, leaving Adrian Lombard, Rolls-Royce's director of engineering, to comment: 'In effect, we have an advanced technical design in search of an aircraft programme.'

Mirroring a repeat occurrence of Rolls-Royce's dances with Boeing on the 707, the 727 and the 747, the ghost of Adrian Lombard would witness the same problem repeating itself on the RB.211 for the DC-10. With the sudden release of the RB.211 from the DC-10, would the highly advanced three-shaft engine have its life curtailed early too? Or would Lockheed insist that the foreign engine company help them?

The Evidence Builds

It is clearly evident from the sources used in this work that a major technology shift occurred with the US aero-engine manufacturers and that the shift was caused by Rolls-Royce's strategy, which was informed by the technologies identified by Conway, Hooker, Lombard, and Dawson et al.

The US engine manufacturers, in their response to Rolls-Royce's total power-plant package, made a paradigm shift in their companies' supply positions, forcing themselves into taking on the responsibility for the complete engine integration with the airframe, providing engine performance guarantees on the wing and supplying a more integrated power-plant package.

The evidence presented here, in my opinion, proves substantially that UK aviation design, engineering processes, technical ability and developed technologies in regards to the power-plant and engine-airframe integration, which were in turn developed for the Airbus A.300, were superior to those respective elements known to and promoted by Boeing and Lockheed for the General Electric and Pratt & Whitney engines on the early 747 and C5A programmes. The evidence presented proves that a crossover of high by-pass turbofan aero-engine technologies occurred between the UK and the US, most probably at inter-government level, which allowed the US aviation industry to apply Rolls-Royce's third generation developments to US McDonnell Douglas DC-10 and Lockheed L1011 second generation wide-bodies.

Significantly, substantial evidence in support of my argument comes from no less an authority than Zeigler himself. In April 1970 Zeigler, the chairman and general manager of SNIAS, the French component of Airbus, noted in an address to the Royal Aeronautical Society's branch at Cranwell: 'It is interesting to observe that the A300B is equipped with powerplants (engines, nacelles, associated equipment), respectively identical to those of the DC-10-30 and L1011.' Newhouse observed: 'Zeigler has a long record of picking the right side of political and industrial issues.'

A comparison between the internal details of the RB.211 (*above left*) and the CF6 (*above right*).
Both engines feature the flared turbine casing indicative of Dawson's aerodynamic gear. (Author)

The GE CF6-6, incorporating the gearbox and accessory drives on the fan cowling. (GE brochure
AEG 5/69-138E via RAeS)

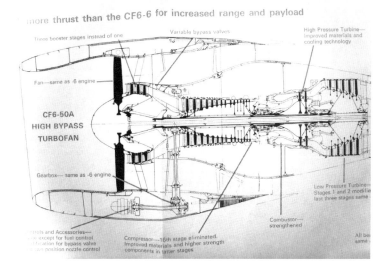

The GE CF6-50A maintained the nacelle and pod of the CF6-6. This diagram from a 1969 brochure highlights the pod bulge in the cool air planar. (GE brochure AEG 6/69-134E via RAeS)

An image of the DC-10 Series 30 from a GE CF6-50A brochure from June 1969. (GE brochure AEG 6/69-134E via RAeS)

American Airlines finally adopts Frank Kolk's high-capacity, high-cycle, twin-engine aircraft in the form of the A.300B.

CHAPTER EIGHTEEN

CONCLUSION:
THE CASE FOR CHANGE

In February 1968, with the imminent prospect of Rolls-Royce being granted the position of the sole supplier of power-plants for both the US McDonnell-Douglas DC-10 and the European Airbus A.300, it appears that such a advantageous position was unacceptable to certain industry and political factions. I suggest that the US administration through the Department of Defense used its financial leverage over Lockheed to ensnare Rolls-Royce in a contract for the L1011. It seems that Lockheed for its part, post-McNamara, would receive a stay of execution and the size of its losses due to program costs over-runs would be reduced to levels bearable to shareholders.

Rolls-Royce was left with no room to bargain with. They had massively committed to the design and development of the 06 series with a forward compressor mounting. With the removal of the American Airlines DC-10 order, Rolls-Royce's untenable position was underscored with the signing of an exclusive engine supply contract for the Lockheed L1011.

Rolls-Royce was beyond the point of no return. With the company's massive commitment of financial and material resources, manpower and several 06 series development engines in build, there was no turning back. Added to this were the onerous financial penalties Lockheed had insisted on putting into the New York court of law contract. Rolls-Royce's neck was firmly in the noose.

Lockheed, once it had Rolls-Royce on board, insisted that the engine supplier would supply no other airframe company with the RB.211. To ensure compliance with Lockheed's demands, the US company insisted that Rolls-Royce re-design the triple-spool high by-pass ratio turbofan around a forward fan case mounting. To complicate matters further, Lockheed insisted that Rolls-Royce brought forward, by at least two years, their plans to provide greater engine thrusts. 'Rolls were tied by very tight performance and delivery conditions which were backed by usurous penalty clauses.' (Hayward)

Because of the meticulous attention to detail that Benn insisted on receiving when Rolls-Royce required state assistance in the form of Launch Aid, Benn would have been very well informed of the potentially drastic consequences of Rolls-Royce entering into sole supply contract with Lockheed. With the changes to the engine that Lockheed insisted on, Benn knew that the financial costs and time costs would severally hamper the British company. Interestingly, Benn did not chastise Rolls-Royce for taking on such an obviously flawed contract, nor did Benn question why UK government funding for the RB.211 was subject to New York law.

Perhaps more indicative of Benn and his ultimate aim for Rolls-Royce was his insistence that 70 per cent launch aid would be provided only for the initial engine development cost forecasts and UK government support was to be limited to a total of £47 million. The additional costs incurred for altering the RB.211 to Lockheed's specific requirements were to be met by the Rolls-Royce company. Benn also agreed to reduce the launching conditions to enable the RB.211 to get onto the L1011. This was something highly unusual as he did not allow the same degree of flexibility for either the DC-10 or the A.300.

The Sting in the Tale

Britain's economic situation in 1968 was desperate. Wilson had little option but to turn to the Americans and the IMF for emergency financial help.

Rolls-Royce's almost-certain success in securing the engine order for the American Airlines DC-10 in early 1968 must have appeared to the blighted British Labour government like a desert oasis. Rolls-Royce's technical success presented the UK Labour government with a political opportunity. An opportunity that would address Labour's determination to end the aviation industry in the UK, provide technical assistance to the US and therefore present a set of circumstances conducive to obtaining a favourable US agreement for financial assistance for the UK.

By going cap in hand to the US and begging for IMF assistance, Wilson effectively delivered the decision making process that would determine the future of the UK's aviation industry into the lap of the US administration. It seems highly probable that the US administration pressured McDonnell-Douglas into replacing the Rolls-Royce RB.211 with the General Electric CF6 engine. Therefore the paper RB.211 had technically won the selection contest for the DC-10.

Unsurprisingly, such a move by the US administration placed Rolls-Royce Limited in a vulnerable negotiating position relative to the only other available US wide-body, the Lockheed L1011. Cross connections between US political interests and their links with the US aviation industry suggest that a manoeuvring of Rolls-Royce Limited into a vulnerable negotiating position was done on purpose, an aim of which was to link Rolls-Royce Limited with Lockheed. This particular aim was achieved with a supply contract for the Rolls-Royce RB.211 on the Lockheed L1011 programme.

Once Rolls-Royce Limited was signed up on the L1011 programme, Lockheed pushed for and secured alterations to the engine contract. These included the movement of the engine mounting from the RB.211's original compressor case mount to a fan case mount. Lockheed also pushed for an increase in the RB.211-06's thrust from 33,620 lbst to 42,000 lbst. Both these post-contract alterations placed the RB.211 in the same category as the GE TF39 turbofan engine for the Lockheed C5A, i.e. front fan case mount and >41,000 lbst thrust.

Therefore, in such a scenario, the design and engineering solutions that Rolls-Royce Limited would have provided, with the redesigned RB.211-22 power-plant and the engine's integration on the L1011, could have been transferred and used by Lockheed in its bid to address US administration concerns on its C5A/TF39 program. Rolls-Royce was most probably positioned to provide Lockheed with technology solutions for a revised TF39 power-plant and engine integration on the C5A and, by extension, the Boeing 747.

The changes demanded by Lockheed also further increased Rolls-Royce Limited's vulnerability by obliging them to proceed with a contract that financially was ultimately impossible for them to adhere to. Gray noted the Pyrrhic victory in *Rolls on the Rocks*: 'For though the public were applauding a triumph Rolls-Royce's head had been forced into a noose.' (Gray 1971)

The position Rolls-Royce Limited found itself in had been fully supported by the British Labour government and by its Minister of Technology Wedgwood Benn, who was very proud of his interesting involvement in Rolls-Royce Limited's success.

In 1966 the British Labour government appointed Anthony Wedgwood Benn as the First Minister of Technology, and it was soon apparent that his decisions were often, to put it politely, curious. His Prime Minister, Harold Wilson, had trumpeted 'the white hot technological revolution'. In total contrast, Benn came to the job with a passionate antipathy for what he called 'technomania', and this applied with particular vehemence to anything emanating from the aircraft industry (unless it was the American aircraft industry).(Gunston 2009)

Interestingly, *The Economist* noted that at the same time that Wedgwood Benn on behalf of the British government proudly acclaimed the Rolls-Royce deal, inspectors from the IMF were scrutinising the British treasury's balance sheets.

At the height of the ATE programme comprising the RB.203 for the FH228, the RB.207 for the Airbus A.300 and the RB.211 for the DC-10, the UK company's future looked assured. However, by the end of 1968 the three-engine programme had been whittled down to just one, the RB.211 for Lockheed.

For Rolls-Royce Limited, betting the company on a technical proposition in a commercial market in the control of the economic hegemon is a daunting prospect; doing the same under political pressure from one's own government and one that is keen to curry favour from the political masters of the hegemon is courting disaster.

Rolls-Royce Limited were either willingly led by Lockheed into providing them with a pylon/cowling solution or unwittingly duped into designing and engineering a solution for the GE TF-39-1 powered Lockheed C-5A.

Referring to the Labour government's Launch Aid package, or the Lockheed L1011, or perhaps both, Sir David Huddie told the DTi investigation: 'We should not have signed that contract.'

BIBLIOGRAPHY

Primary Sources

Rolls-Royce: Technical

TSD.1226, *Rolls-Royce RB.141 By-Pass Turbo Jet* (Derby: Rolls-Royce Limited, May 1959).

TSD.1214 *Rolls-Royce Conway By-Pass Turbo Jet* (2nd edn, Derby: Rolls-Royce Limited, June 1959).

TS.252, Issue 3, *A Presentation of The Rolls-Royce TRENT* (Derby: Rolls-Royce Limited, February 1967).

TS.298, *RB.207 Technical Description* (Rolls-Royce Limited, March 1968).

Bristol Siddeley: Technical

P.S.225, Bristol Siddeley – SNECMA, *BS 123 Series of High BY-PASS Ratio Engines* (July 1965).

BSS.49, SNECMA – Bristol Siddeley, *Proposal for the Powerplant for the European Airbus* (February 1967).

Historical

Airbus, *A300 B* (Airbus Brochure No. 2, 1970)

Allward, Maurice, 'Europe's A300 Airbus' in *Air Pictorial* (London, May 1974).

Bristol Siddeley, *This is Bristol Siddeley* TJ 123 (London: Cond, 1961).

Bristol Quarterly, 'Two Spool Turbojet. The Olympus: A New Kind of Jet Engine' in *Bristol Engines* Vol. 1 (Winter 1953).

Brown, D. L., MIMechE, AMICE, MIGasE, AFRAeS, 'The Origin of the Bypass and Ducted Fan' in *The Aeroplane*, 13 March 1959, pp. 313–316.

Dawson, L., chief engineer (projects) Rolls-Royce Ltd, 'Engines for Advanced Subsonic Transports' in *Flight International*, 7 January 1965, pp. 22–23.

Eltis, E. M., 'Mr. Lombard's leadership on the evolution of the three-shaft engine' in *Roll-Royce News*, 10 April 1968.

Eltis, E. and Morley, F. W., 'Short Haul Engine Economics' in *Flight*, 22 October 1964.

Finletter, T., *Survival In The Air Age: A Report by the President's Air Policy Commission* (Washington: United States Government Printing Office, 1 January 1948).

Green, William, editorial director, 'Europe's Airbus' in *Flying Review International* (London: Purnell, October 1967).

Hawker Siddeley Aviation, *A300B* HSA hat/SE/3023/KB/A300B (August 1970).

Hawker Siddeley Aviation, *A Presentation of the HS132* (Hatfield: Hawker Siddeley Aviation Limited, circa 1965).

Lewis, Dr G. M., '50 Years of Jet-Powered Flight: The Evolution Of The By-Pass Engine'. A paper to be presented at the DGLR-Symposium, Munich 26 to 27 October 1989 (Rolls-Royce plc).

Lombard, A. A. and Gerdan D., 'Turbofans and By-Pass Type Engines for Jet Transports'. SAE paper, New York, 8 April 1960. Reprinted in *Flight* 8 April 1960.

Lombard, A. A. 'Jet Engine Trends'. A paper at the International Congress on Air Technology given at Hot Springs, Arkansas, USA, in November 1965. *Flight International*, 30 December 1965, pp. 1,116–1,119.

Lombard, A. A., and Hewson, Dr C. T., 'From Whittle to 1997' in *Flight*, 27 April 1967.

Lord Plowden, *Report of the Committee of Enquiry into the Aircraft Industry* (London: Cmnd 2853, HMSO, December 1965).

Lord Plowden, *Flight*, 10 March 1966.

McRae, D. M., 'The Aerodynamic development of the A-300B wing'. RAeS lecture, Hatfield, 8 February 1972. Published in *Flight International*, 10 February 1972.

Middleton, Peter and Marsden, John, 'European Airbus: A-300B'. *Flight International* Special Report, 6 April 1972.

Morley, F. W., chief design engineer, Rolls-Royce Ltd, 'A Philosophy of Aircraft Engine Manufacture'. Sempill Paper, circa 1964, pp. 2–16.

Rolls-Royce Aero Engines, *Thirty Seven Years of Aero Engines* (Derby: Rolls-Royce Limited, 1951).

SNECMA/Bristol Siddeley, *Proposal for the Powerplant for the European Airbus* BSS 49 (February 1967).

Whittle, F., Air Commodore, 'The Whittle Jet Propulsion Gas Turbine' in *The Engineer*, 12 October 1945.

Whittle, Sir Frank, *Jet: The Story Of A Pioneer* (London: Pan, 1957)

Whittle, Sir Frank. 'A Brief Summary of Power Jets' Work on Turbofans' in Golley and Gunston, *Genesis of the Jet* (Shrewsbury: Airlife, 1997).

Wilde, G. L. and Pickerell, D. J., 'The Rolls-Royce Three Shaft Turbo-Fan Engine'. Rolls-Royce, Derby. Paper presented to the American Institute of Aeronautics and Astronautics Commercial Aircraft Design and Operation Meeting, 1967.

Wood, Derek, 'The British Aircraft Industry 1968' in *Interavia*, September 1968.

General

Flight International
Various, inc:
'Turbofans'. *Flight* 30 October 1959
Flight International 26 November 1964
Flight International 24 February 1966

Flight International 3 March 1966
Flight International 19 May 1966.
'Rolls-Royce Tomorrow'. *Flight International* 21 July 1966

The Aeroplane
Air Pictorial
The Daily Telegraph
The Economist
The Rolls-Royce Magazine
The Times
The Wall Street Journal
The Engineer
Air International
Flying Review
Interavia
Rolls-Royce News
AWST
Science News
Time

Hansard
The Minister of Aviation Supply (Mr Frederick Corfield), 'Rolls-Royce (Launching Aid)'. *Hansard*, Commons Sitting 23 November 1970, 9.31 p.m.

The Fleet Air Arm Museum at Yeovilton, Somerset

Scientific

Royal Society
Lombard, A. A., 'Aircraft power plants-past, present and future', First Society Technology Lecture in *Royal Society* Vol. 298. A. (28 March 1967).
Royal Aeronautical Society: The Aeronautical Journal
Armstrong, J. P. and Jones, A. T., 'The Advantages of Three-Shaft Turbofan Engines for Civil Transport Operation' in *The Aeronautical Journal of the Royal Aeronautical Society*, Vol. 73 (January 1969).
Bennett, H. W., 'The development of the composite material engine nacelle' in *The Aeronautical Journal of the Royal Aeronautical Society* (July 1980).
Brown, D. G., chief project engineer, Hawker Siddeley Aviation Ltd, Hatfield, 'After Concorde and the Airbus what follows?' in *The Aeronautical Journal of the Royal Aeronautical Society*, Vol. 73 (May 1969), p. 397.
Davies, Handel, 'Some Thoughts about the Future of European Aeronautics' in *The Aeronautical Journal of the Royal Aeronautical Society*, Vol. 72 (May 1968).
Dawson, L. G. and Holliday, J. B., 'Propulsion' in *The Aeronautical Journal of The Royal Aeronautical Society*, Vol. 72 (September 1968).
Edwards, John. L., 'By the Application of Power' in *The Aeronautical Journal of The Royal Aeronautical Society*, Vol.79 (February 1975).

Frisbee, L. E., 'The Lockheed Tristar – An Operational Overview' in *The Aeronautical Journal of The Royal Aeronautical Society* (September 1974).

Hooker, S. G., 'The Engine Scene' in *The Aeronautical Journal of The Royal Aeronautical Society*, Vol. 74 (January 1970).

Huddie, Sir David, 'Economics of Propulsion Systems for Air Transport' in *The Aeronautical Journal of the Royal Aeronautical Society*, Vol. 74 (June 1970).

Lloyd, Peter, 'Engine Development Under the Ministry of Aviation' in *The Aeronautical Journal of The Royal Aeronautical Society*, Vol. 72 (February 1968).

Pearson, J. D., chief executive and deputy chairman, Rolls-Royce Ltd, 'A Review of the Aero Engine Industry in the West Since the End of the Second World War' in *The Journal of the Royal Aeronautical Society*, Vol. 66, No. 619 (July 1962).

Robinson, P. and Brown, D. G., 'Short haul transport for the 1990s' in *The Aeronautical Journal of the Royal Aeronautical Society* (November 1979).

Ruffles, P. C., 'Aero engines of the future' in *The Aeronautical Journal of the Royal Aeronautical Society* (June 2003).

Smith, J. P., director and chief engineer, civil, Hawker Siddeley Aviation Ltd. 'The Development of the Trident Series' in *The Aeronautical Journal of the Royal Society*, Vol. 73 (November 1969).

Wilde, G. L., chief engineer – advanced projects, Rolls-Royce Ltd, Derby, 'Future large civil turbofans and powerplants' in *The Aeronautical Journal of the Royal Aeronautical Society*, Vol. 82 (July 1978).

Ziegler, H., 'The Major Development Trends in Air Transport and European Co-operation' in *The Aeronautical Journal of The Royal Aeronautical Society*, Vol. 75 (May 1970).

IMechE

Eltis, E. M. and Wilde, G. L., 'The Rolls-Royce RB211 Turbofan Engine', The James Clayton Lecture in *Proceedings Institute Mechanical Engineers*, Vol. 188, 37/74 (1974).

Singh, Riti, 'Civil Aero Gas Turbines: Technology and Strategy', Chairman's Address, Aerospace Industries Division, Cranfield University, 24 April 2001, pp. 1–19.

Whittle, Air Commodore F., 'The Early History of the Whittle Jet Propulsion Gas Turbine', the First James Clayton Lecture in *Proceedings Institute Mechanical Engineers*, Vol. 152, 419/435 (1945).

Whyte, R. R., *Engineering Progress Through Trouble* (1975).

Physics in Science

Dykins, Donald H., 'A Wing for the Airbus', published in *Physics in Technology*, November 1976.

SAE

Blunt, A. and Lupton, J. R., 'Installation Features of Rolls-Royce Advanced Technology Transport Engines'. Rolls-Royce Limited. *SAE*, February 1968/9?.

Jackson, H. A. and Pohlman, H., 'JT9D Engine Operating Experience' in *SAE* 700288 (1970).

Krebs, James N. and Kappus, Peter G., 'Advanced Military Transport Engines' in *SAE* 700267 (1970).

Pearson, Harry, 'The Development of Propulsion Systems for Air Transport' in *SAE* 720598 (1972).

Sens, William. H. and Meyer, Robert M., 'Military/Commercial Aircraft Propulsion Relationships' in *SAE* 700268 (National Air Transport Meeting, New York, NY, April 20-23 1970).

Thompson, J. R. and Smith, M. J. T., 'Minimum Noise Pod Design' in *SAE* 700805 (1970).

AIAA

MacKinnon, M. I. K. and Mehta, B. K., 'Factors Influencing Nacelle Design on 747', Boeing Commercial Airplane Co., Seattle, Washington. AIAA/SAE/ASME 15th Joint Propulsion Conference. Las Vegas, June 18-20, 1979.

Sussman, Mark. B. 'A Remark Concerning Engine-Inlet Distortion', The Boeing Company. Seattle, in *AIAA J. Aircraft*, Vol. 5, No. 1, Jan-Feb. 1968, pp. 95–96.

Wilde, G. L. and Pickerell, D. J. 'The Rolls-Royce Three Shaft Turbo-Fan Engine'. Rolls-Royce, Derby, 1967. Paper presented to the American Institute of Aeronautics and Astronautics Commercial Aircraft Design and Operation Meeting.

UK Aeronautical Research Council

Reports and Memoranda

Bagley, J. A. and Kurn, A. G. *Jet Interference on Supercritical Wings*. Procurement Executive, Ministry of Defence, Aerodynamics Department, RAE, Farnborough, Hants. HMSO London, R&M No. 3845, 1977.

Bridle, E. A. *Assessment of the Relative Performance of the By-pass Engine and the Orthodox Double Compound Jet Engine*. Ministry of Supply, HMSO, London, R&M No. 2862, July 1948.

Secondary Sources and Resources

Alford, B. W. E., *Britain in the World Economy since 1880* (London: Longman, 1996).

Badrocke, Mike and Gunston, Bill, *Lockheed Aircraft Cutaways* (London: Osprey, 1998).

Banks, Air Commodore Rodwell, *I Kept No Diary* (Shrewsbury: Airlife, 1978).

Barfield, Norman, *Broughton: From Wellington to Airbus* (Stroud: Tempus, 2001).

Barnett, Correlli, *The Verdict of Peace* (London: Macmillan, 2001).

Battlehouse. Concorde End of An Era. Duke Video. Douglas IoM. 2009

Bauer, Martin W., and Bucchi, Massimiano (eds), *Journalism, Science and Society* (London: Routledge, 2007).

Baxter, Alan, 'The BS75 Family' in Bristol Branch "Sleeve Notes", Rolls-Royce Heritage Trust, May 1999.pp.34-40.

Berry, Peter, 'The Development of Early Turbojet Engines' in *Air-Britain Digest*, Winter 2001, pp. 164–167.

Berry, Peter, *Turbojet Engines: The Low-Bypass Turbofans* (Aviation World, 2003).

Beteille, Roger, 'The Basic Strategy of Airbus' in *The Putnam Aeronautical Review*, Issue Seven (September 1990).

Bittlingmayer, George,' Property, Progress, and the Aircraft Patent Agreement' in *Journal of Law and Economics*, Vol. 31, No. 1 (April 1988), pp. 227-248.

Blake, John, *Flight: The Five Ages of Aviation* (London: Guild Publishing, 1987).

Bülkow. Ludwig, 'Anticipating the future...' interview conducted by Manfred Knappe in *Planet Aerospace*, issue No. 7 (2002).

Boulton, David, *The Lockheed Papers* (London: Cape, 1978).

Bowden, Sue, 'Ownership Responsibilities and Corporate Governance: The Crisis at Rolls-Royce, 1968–71' in *Business History*, Vol. 44, No. 3 (2002), pp.31-62.

Bowman, Martin W., *The Encyclopedia of US Military Aircraft* (London: Arms and Armour Press, 1980).

Boyne, Walter J., Beyond the Horizons (New York: St Martins, 1998).

Boyne, Walter J. and Lopez, Donald S. (eds), *The Jet Age: Forty Years of Jet Aviation* (Washington: Smithsonian Institution Press, 1979).

Boyne, Walter J., *The Leading Edge* (New York: Artabras, 1991).

Bramson, Alan, *Pure Luck: The Authorized Biography of Sir Thomas Sopwith, 1888–1989* (Wellingborough: Patrick Stephens Ltd, 1990).

British Aviation Preservation Council. Aero-Engines Exhibited & Stored in the United Kingdom & Ireland. C. 2005

British Library.

Brook, Peter W., *The Modern Airliner: Its Origins and Development* (London: Putnam, 1961).

Brooks, David, Vikings At Waterloo. Rolls-Royce Heritage Trust. Historical Series No.22. Derby. 1997

Brown, Derek, 'Airbus: The Formative Years' in *The Putnam Aeronautical Review*, Issue Seven (September 1990).

Brown, Derek, 'Airbus: Expanding the Product Range' in *The Putnam Aeronautical Review*, Issue Seven (September 1990).

Brown, Captain Eric, *Miles M.52: Gateway to Supersonic Flight* (Stroud: Spellmount, 2012).

Butler, Tony, *British Secret Projects – Jet Bombers Since 1949* (Hinckley: Midland Publishing, 2003).

Canadian Broadcasting Corporation. There Never Was an Arrow. Executive Producer Paul Wright (Film) 1979

Cole, Lance, *Vickers VC10* (Marlborough: Crowood Press, 2000).

Cooper, Peter J., *Farnborough: 100 Years of British Aviation* (Hinckley: Midland Publishing, 2006).

Connors, Jack, *The Engines of Pratt & Whitney: A Technical History* (Raston, VA: American Institute of Aeronautics and Aerospace, 2010).

Coplin, J. F., *Aircraft Jet Engines* (Macdonald & Co., 1967).

Coplin, John F., 'Technology of the Rolls-Royce RB.211 Engine' in *The Rolls-Royce Magazine* 1 (June–August 1979) pp. 27–33.

Coplin, John F., Interview recorded at RR Derby in 2011. British Library sound Archives (RB&MS). Accessed 26 April 2012.

Costello, John and Hughes, Terry, *Concorde* (London: Angus & Robertson, 1976).

Cownie, J. R., 'Success Through Perseverance: The Rolls-Royce RB.211 Engine' in *The Putnam Aeronautical Review*, Issue Four (December 1989).

Cowney, Jim, 'Rolls-Royce's Big Fan' in *Civil Aviation Review* (London: Aircraft Illustrated Ian Allan, 1990).

Cotter, Jarrod (ed.), *Avro Vulcan* (Horncastle: Aviation Classics, Mortons, 2010).

Crosby, Francis, *The World Encyclopedia of Bombers* (London: Hermes House, 2004).

DD Home Entertainment. TSR2 The Untold Story. (DVD) DD Home Entertainment 2005

Darling, Kev, *Concorde* (Marlborough: Crowood. 2004).

Donne, Michael, *Leader of the Skies* (London: Frederick Muller, 1981).

Dow, Andrew, *Pegasus: The Heart of the Harrier* (Barnsley: Pen & Sword, 2009).

Eden, Paul E. (gen. ed.), *Civil Aircraft Today* (Leicester: Silverdale, 2006).

Francillon, Rene, *McDonnell Douglas Aircraft Since 1920* (London: Putnam, 1979).

Gallagher, Brendan (ed.), *Illustrated History of Aircraft* (London: Octopus, 1977)

Gardner, Charles, *British Aircraft Corporation* (London: Batsford, 1981).

General Electric. CF6 High Bypass Turbofan. AEG 5/69-138E. G.E. 1969

General Electric. CF6-50A High Bypass Turbofan. AEG 6/69-134E. G.E. 1969

Gilchrist, Peter, *Boeing 747* (Shepperton: Ian Allan, 1999).

Gray, Robert, *Rolls on the Rocks* (Salisbury: Panther, 1971).

Green, Geoff, *British Aerospace: A Proud Heritage* (Geoff Green, 1988).

Green, William and Pollinger, Gerald, *The Observer's Book of Aircraft* (London: Warne, 1952).

Green, William and Pollinger, Gerald, *The Observer's Book of Aircraft* (London: Warne, 1957).

Green, William and Pollinger, Gerald, *The Observer's Book of Aircraft* (London: Warne, 1958).

Green, William and Pollinger, Gerald, *The Observer's Book of Aircraft* (London: Warne, 1959).

Green, William and Pollinger, Gerald, *The Observer's Book of Aircraft* (London: Warne, 1960).

Green, William and Punnett, Dennis, *The Observer's Book of Basic Aircraft: Civil* (London: Warne, 1967).

Green, William and Punnett, Dennis, *The Observer's Book of Basic Aircraft: Military* (London: Warne, 1967).

Gunston, Bill, *The Jet Age* (London: Arthur Baker Limited, 1971).

Gunston, W. T., 'Developments in Aircraft and Missiles' in *Brassey's Annual* (London, 1972) pp. 268–269.

Gunston, Bill, *Airbus: The European Triumph* (London: Osprey, 1988).

Gunston, Bill, *Rolls-Royce Aero Engines* (Sparkford: Patrick Stephens Limited, 1989).

Gunston, Bill, *Plane Speaking* (Sparkford: Patrick Stephens Limited, 1991).

Gunston, Bill, *World Encyclopaedia of Aero Engines* (Stroud: Sutton, 2006).

Gunston, Bill, *The Development of Jet And Turbine Aero Engines* (4th edn, Sparkford: Patrick Stephens Limited, 2007).

Gunston, Bill, *Airbus: The Complete Story* (Yeovilton: Haynes, 2009).

Hamilton-Paterson, James, *Empire of the Clouds* (London: Faber and Faber, 2010).

Harker, R. W., OBE, *Rolls-Royce From the Wings* (Oxford Illustrated Press, 1976).

Harker, Ronald, *The Engines Were Rolls-Royce* (New York: Macmillan, 1979).

Hartley, Michael, *The Rolls-Royce Spey* (Derby: Rolls-Royce Heritage Trust Technical Series No. 10, 2008).

Hastings, Stephen, *The Murder of TSR-2* (London: MacDonald, 1966).

Hayward, Keith, 'Politics and European Aero-Space Collaboration: The A300 Airbus' in *The Journal of Common Market Studies* 14 Part 4 (1976) pp. 354–367.

Hayward, Keith, *Government and British Civil Aerospace* (1983).

Heppenheimer.T.A. SP-4221 The Space Shuttle Decision: NASA's Search for a Reusable Space Vehicle. NASA History Office, Office of Policy and Plans, Washington, D.C. 1999 updated by Steven J. Dick, NASA Chief Historian, 6 Aug 2004

Heppenheimer, T. A., *Turbulent Skies: The History of Commercial Aviation* (New York: John Wiley & Sons, Inc., 1995).

Hood, Edward E., *Commercial Aircraft Engines by General Electric* (Interavia).

Hooker, Sir Stanley, *Not Much of an Engineer* (Airlife, 1984).

Hooker, S. G., *From Merlin to Pegasus* (1975).

Hooks, Michael J. (ed.), *Airbus A300 in Aviation Year* (London: Avia, 1978).

Howse, Mike (director, engineering and technology, Rolls-Royce Plc), 'Aero Gas Turbines – An ever changing engineering challenge', Whittle Lecture, Royal Aeronautical Society, London (February 2004).

Hughes, Thomas P., *Rescuing Prometheus* (New York: Pantheon, 1998).

Hunecke, Klaus, *Jet Engines* (1997).

Ince, Martin, *The Politics of British Science* (Brighton: Wheatsheaf, 1986).

Jackson, Robert, *Cold War Combat Prototypes* (Marlborough: Crowood Press, 2005).

Jane's All The World's Aircraft 1966–67 (Jane's, 1966).

Jones, R. V., *Most Secret War* (Wordsworth: Ware, 1998).

Knaack, Marcelle Size., *Military Airlift and Aircraft Procurement: The Case of the C-5A* (Washington, D.C.: Air Force History & Museums Program, 1998).

Kermode, A. C., *Flight Without Fomulae* (5th edn, updated by Bill Gunston, Longman: Harlow, 1989).

Lawrence, Philip K. and Thornton, David W., *Deep Stall* (Ashgate, 2005).

Lazonik. William., and Prencipe. Andrea., Dynamic capabilities and sustained
innovation: strategic control and financial commitment at Rolls-Royce plc. Industrial and Corporate Change Advance Access published May 9, Oxford University Press. 2005

Lironi, Paolo, *The Engine Yearbook* (2007).

Lynch, Frances and Johnman, Lewis, 'Technological Non-Cooperation: Britain and Airbus, 1965-1969' in *Journal of European Integration History*, Vol. 12, No. 1 (2006).

Lynn, Matthew, *Birds of Prey* (1995).

MacCrindle, R. A. and Godfrey, P., *Rolls-Royce Limited* (London: Department of Trade and Industry, 1973).

Magruder, William F. (director, SST development program), 'After the SST, Where do we go?' in *Automotive Engineering*, Vol. 80, No. 1 (January 1972), pp.81–91.

McGowen, Jackson R. (president and chief executive officer, Douglas Aircraft Co.), 'After the SST, Where do we go?' in *Automotive Engineering*, Vol. 80, No. 1 (January 1972), pp.81–91.

McKenzie, A., Axial Compressor Development At Rolls-Royce Derby, 1946-1962. TS.11. Rolls-Royce Heritage Trust, Derby. 2009

McKim, Dr Frank, *Trident: A History* (Stroud: The History Press, 2008).

Mowrey, David C., *Alliance Politics and Economics* (1987).

Museum of Science and Industry, Manchester.

NASA History Office (www.history.nasa.gov).

Nelson, Donald Alfred, 'Concorde: International Cooperation in Aviation' in *The American Journal of Comparative Law*, Vol. 17, No. 3 (1969), pp. 452–467.

Newhouse, John, *The Sporty Game* (New York: Knopf, 1982).

Nibloe, Max, 'Performance and Prospects' in *Interavia*, September 1970.

Nockolds, Harold, *The Magic of a Name*, (London: Foulis, 1959).

Owen, Geoffrey, *From Empire to Europe* (London: Harper Collins, 1999).

Owen, Kenneth, 'RB211: Growing pains of a special engine' in *Design Journal*, Issue 306 (June 1974), pp. 72-75.

Ower, E. and Nayler, J., *High Speed Flight* (London: Hutchinson, 1956).

Payne, Richard, *Stuck on the Drawing Board* (Stroud: Tempus, 2004).

Payzer, R. J., 'Development of the General Electric CF6 turbofan' in *Interavia*, March 1969.

Pearson, Harry, *Rolls-Royce and the Rateau Patents* (Derby: Rolls-Royce Heritage Trust Technical Series No. 1, 1989).

Pelletier, Alain, *Boeing: The Complete Story* (Yeovil: Haynes, 2010).

Ponting, Clive, *Breach of Promise* (London: 1989).

Pugh, Peter, *The Magic of a Name* Part Two (Duxford: Icon, 2001).

Pugh, Peter, *The Magic of a Name* Part Three (Duxford: Icon, 2002).

Pugh, Peter and Howie, David, *Rolls-Royce 1904-2004: A Century of Innovation* (Rolls-Royce Plc, 2004).

RAF Museum Cosford.

RAF Museum Hendon.

Reed, Arthur, *Britain's Aircraft Industry* (London: Dent, 1973).

Roberson, Dr E. C. The True Book About Jet Engines and Gas Turbines (London: Muller, 1961).

Roger Louis, Wm, 'The Dissolution of the British Empire' in Roger Louis, Wm and Brown, Judith (eds), *The Oxford History of The British Empire: Volume IV: The Twentieth Century* (Oxford University Press, 1999).

Rolls-Royce plc, *The Jet Engine* (4th edn, Derby, 1986).

Rolls-Royce Heritage Trust Bristol.

Rolls-Royce Heritage Trust Derby.

Rowe, Brian H. and Ducheny, Martin, *The Power to Fly* (Barnsley, 2005).

Roy, Raj, *No Secrets Between 'Special friends': America's involvement in British economic Policy, October 1964 – April 1965* (Oxford: The Historical Association and Blackwell Publishing, 2004).

Royal Aeronautical Society Library, Farnborough.

Science Museum. South Kensington, London.

Scranton, Philip, 'Urgency, uncertainty, and innovation: Building jet engines in postwar America' in *Management & Organizational History* Vol. 1 (2) (2006), pp127-157.

Serling, Robert J., *The Jet Age* (Virginia: Time Life Books, 1982).

Singfield, Tom, *Classic Airliners* (Leicester: Midland Publishing, 2000).

Skidelsky, Robert, *John Maynard Keynes* (London: Pan Macmillan, 2004).

Skinner, Stephen, *BAC One-Eleven: The Whole Story* (Stroud: Tempus, 2002).

St Peter, James, *The History of Aircraft Gas Turbine Engine Development in the United States... A tradition of excellence* (Atlanta, Georgia: International Gas Turbine Institute of the American Society of Mechanical Engineers, 1999).

Steiner, John E., 'Jet Aviation Development: A Company Perspective' in Boyne, W. and Lopez, D. (eds), *The Jet Age* (Washington: Smithsonian, 1979).

Stevens, James Hay, *The How and Why of the By-Pass Engine* (Air Pictorial, 1952).

Stevens, James Hay, *The Shape of the Aeroplane* (London: Hutchinson, 1953).

Stroud, John, *The World's Airliners* (London: The Bodley Head, 1975).

Stuart, Charles, 'The US-Europe Airline Industry Gap' in *Interavia*, October 1968.

Taylor, John W. R. (ed.), *Jane's All the World's Aircraft 1966–67* (London: Sampson Low, Marston & Co., 1966).

Taylor, John W. R., *Aircraft Aircraft* (London: Hamlyn, 1970).

Taylor, John W. R. and Swanborough, Gordon, *Civil Aircraft of the World* (London: Ian Allan, 1974).

Taylor, John W. R. and Swanborough, Gordon, *Military Aircraft of the World* (London: Ian Allan, 1979).

Thad Allen, Michael and Hecht, Gabrielle (eds.), *Technologies of Power* (Massachusetts: MIT Press, 2001).

Thornborough, Anthony, *British Aircraft Corporation T S R 2* (2nd edn, Ringshall: An Aeroguide Special, Ad Hoc Publications, 2006).

Thornton, David Weldon, *Airbus Industrie* (London: Macmillan, 1995).

Warner, Guy, *Shorts – The Foreman Years* (Belfast: Ulster Aviation Society, 2008).

Wilde, Geoffrey, *Flow matching of the stages of Axial Compressors* (Derby: Rolls-Royce Heritage Trust Technical Series No.4, 1999).

Wilson, T. A. (president and chief executive officer, Boeing Co.), 'After the SST, Where do we go?' in *Automotive Engineering*, Vol. 80, No. 1 (January 1972), pp.81–91.

Wood, Derek, *Project Cancelled: A searching criticism of the abandonment of Britain's advanced aircraft projects* (London: Macdonald and Jane's, 1975).

Wright, Alan J., *Airbus* (London: Ian Allan, 1984).

Yenne, Bill, *Lockheed* (London: Bison, 1987).

ACKNOWLEDGEMENTS

This book could never have existed without the valiant efforts and sterling work of all the brave and loyal men and women who once proudly worked in Britain's aviation industries. To you all I give my utmost thanks.

I wish to thank Bob Hercock and Patrick Hassell and all of Rolls-Royce Heritage Trust Bristol. Also thanks to Ian Craighead and Anna and all at Rolls-Royce Heritage Trust Derby.

My thanks are given to John Eaver of Royal Aeronautical Society Bristol and to all the great and knowledgeable people I have met on his tours. Thanks to Brian Russel and Christine at RAeS National Aerospace Library at Farnborough and to all at the Royal Aeronautical Society London.

I especially want to thank the many wonderful museums I have visited, in particular the RAF museums at Cosford and Hendon and the Museum of Science and Industry in Manchester. To Nick Forder and all at MoSI, thank you.

Thanks also to my friends at Avro Lancashire. Thanks to Campbell and louis and all at Amberley Publishing.

Finally, I would like to thank my family, without whose untiring and unwavering support my efforts would have come to naught. Thanks to my mother Carol and my father Edmund, to my sister Sarah and to all my family. I thank you for your patience.

I hope I have been a faithful servant of history and that I have learned from the past to make good my future. To my daughters Francesca and Annabelle, my best wishes and God be with you.

Andrew

CREDITS

All the sources credited in the Bibliography have been referred to and all quotes originate from the sources.

All pictures are the author's via R-RHT and the museums. Where copyright has been established it is acknowledged. I apologise in advance should you find a picture which is your work and unatrributed to you – please contact me.

All mistakes and omissions are mine.

Andrew

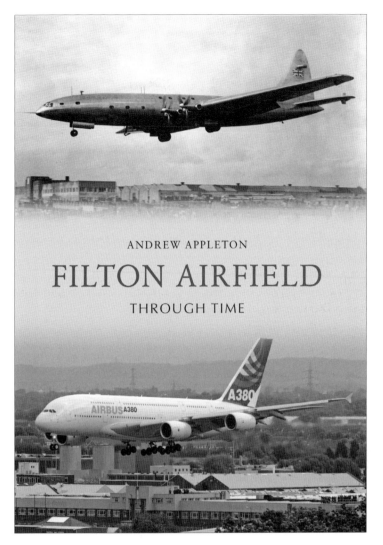

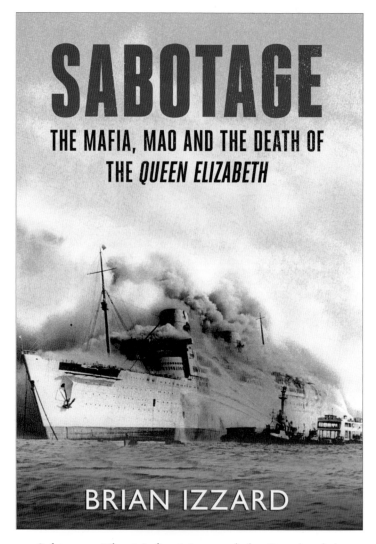

Sabotage: The Mafia, Mao and the Death of the
Queen Elizabeth

Brian Izzard

A detective story of the highest order, telling the story leading up to
the arson and destruction of the Cunard liner RMS *Queen Elizabeth*.

978 1 4456 0348 3
224 pages

Available from all good bookshops or order direct
from our website www.amberleybooks.com